The Weiser Field Guide to
vampires

Legends, Practices, and Encounters
Old and New

J. M. Dixon

WEISERBOOKS
San Francisco, CA / Newburyport, MA

First published in 2009 by
Red Wheel/Weiser, LLC
With offices at:
500 Third Street, Suite 230
San Francisco, CA 94107
www.redwheelweiser.com

ISBN: 978-1-57863-449-1
Library of Congress Cataloging-in-Publication Data
is available upon request.

Typeset in Jenson and Priori Sans.

Images on pages 12, 18, 20, 21, 22, 23, 28, 32, 37, 40,
42, 44, 47, 48, 49, 50, 51, 58, 65, 67, 68, 71, 75, 75, 84,
87, 89, 95, 96, 99, 102, 106, 108, 113, 117, 119, 120,
121, 126, 135, 147, 151, 154, 163 © Dreamstime.
Images on pages 27, 33, 35, 56, 66, 73, 127, 132,
139, 160 © iStockphoto. Images on pages 38, 54, 104
© Miss Mary's. Image on page 17 © Veer.
Images on pages 83 and 158 © Pepin Press.

Printed in Canada
TCP
10 9 8 7 6 5 4 3 2 1

The paper used in this publication meets the minimum
requirements of the American National Standard for
Information Sciences—Permanence of Paper for
Printed Library Materials Z39.48-1992 (R1997).

This book is dedicated to my beautiful Nada, who has done more than I ever could have asked to help this book be what it is. I owe her my heart, my thanks, and much more.

Contents

Introduction

From the very beginning, this book was intended to be everything the reader needs to know about the world of vampires, refined and condensed into a compact, pocket-sized format. Much has changed since this project began, with much added and even more cut away, but the focus and original goal have stayed the same. This text remains a fat-free, end-all, be-all field guide to the lives, worlds, and existences of vampires.

However, the vampires that exist within may not be exactly what the reader is expecting. The modern person's idea of a vampire is most often based upon the romantic fictions of fine writers like Anne Rice, Stephenie Meyer, Poppy Z. Brite, and, of course, Bram Stoker, as well as modern movies like the *Blade* series and television shows like the ever-famous *Buffy the Vampire Slayer* and its counterpart, *Angel,* or the new HBO series *True Blood;* but these are not the only vampires discussed in this book. The many vampires throughout history exist in forms modern minds rarely conceive, such as the body-jumping spirits called *khakhua* by the Krowai people of Papua New Guinea and the *loogaroo* of Grenada, who shed their flesh at night to hunt human prey as balls of flame.

This book is devoted to those creatures of modern and ancient myth and to one more that bridges the gap between the two, having possibly been the origin of both. Also known as *Strigoi Vii, Vampyres,* and *Human Living Vampires*, these modern vampires share much in common with their fictitious counterparts, though they make no claims to being immortal or the living dead. Instead, these creatures have a firm grip on reality and their own humanity while simultaneously living with the knowledge that they have other needs that are greatly beyond the human, needs that they sate through feeding on the blood or the psychic energy of humans.

The Weiser Field Guide to Vampires was written to give the average reader a window into the worlds of these beings of myth, fantasy, reality, and everywhere the lines between them blur. It is intended to cut a path through these deep and dark woods so anyone can see both the beauty and the horror of the vampire with his or her own eyes. Within are things born not only of the subconscious fears of humanity but also from that which is incomprehensible to the modern man. So please proceed with caution, awe, and, most of all, an open mind.

In the end, vampires throughout history have been creatures both sought after and feared. People hear the mythologies and tales and wonder about the truth behind them. Hopefully, this book will help the reader sort through the fictions, the fantasies, the truths, the histories, and a bit of everything in between. For those interested in going into the night in search of vampires for themselves, keep your eyes open, your mind sharp, and never ever forget your field guide.

CHAPTER I

The Vampiric World

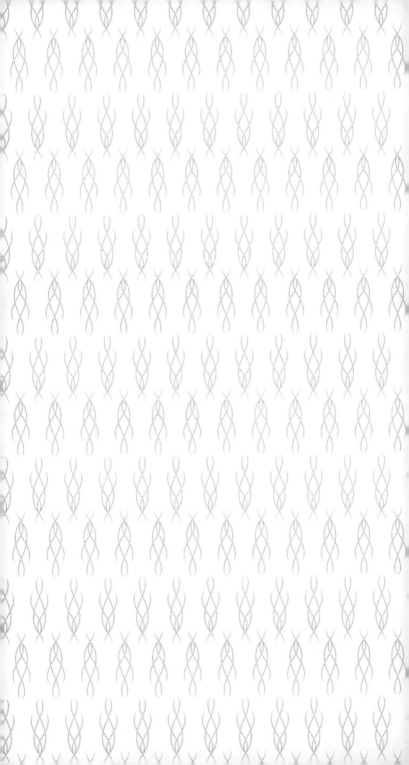

Over the many millennia of its existence, humanity has developed and grown by leaps and bounds, but always under the watchful eyes of certain "others." Human art, architecture, literature, and even technology have all been influenced by these creatures as they have both led the human world and followed in its shadow. Though they go by many names, the most common one used today is simply *vampire*. Whether they are reviled or revered, the world cannot be rid of them, for stories of their kind have haunted humanity through the entire course of recorded history, culminating in a modern age in which every medium of entertainment is dominated by their influence—from literature to television, from the vastly popular novels of Anne Rice to children's programs like *Sesame Street*, with its Count character. Novels, horror movies, and scary video games with vampires—not to mention gothic, punk, and rock music—are all creations of this new vampire age. But these fictions tell only half the story.

Celtic Vampires

Take, for instance, the Celtic legends of the Sidhe. Ancient and modern historians alike find these legends to be at least in part true histories of the ancient peoples of Ireland. The ranks of those historians have included the monks that recorded the only existing copies of these legends of the wars and lineage of the first races of Ireland as well as the Victorian writer Elizabeth A. Gray, who translated the history of the

Second Battle of Mag Tuired into English. This history records the political and military struggles between the Tuatha De Danaan, a race of powerful human magickal practitioners and warriors, and the Fomoire, the warrior caste of the Sidhe—*Sidhe* being the Celtic word for what today are called vampires. According to these histories, the Sidhe once dominated Ireland, existing in such great numbers that there were armies of them.

According to Celtic legend, the Sidhe were one of  the oldest peoples of Ireland, having emigrated there from a faraway land. Existing in relative peace and harmony with various other peoples that passed through the land, these people opened their territories freely to the Tuatha De Danaan. Conflict arose between these two peoples, and war broke out.

According to Gray's translation, the Tuatha De Danaan were fully aware that a fight with these powerful and intelligent beings would amount to group suicide. (In fact, Gray's translation likens such an act to thrusting one's hand into an asp's nest or dashing one's head against a cliff.) So the Tuatha De Danaan used their powers to put four curses upon the Sidhe. Only two seem to have worked: one that would cause the light of day to scorch their skin and burn their eyes, and one that would allow no water to quench their thirst. Although in the end the Tuatha De Danaan won the battle, they lived in fear that they had created monsters that would eventually destroy them.

The Tuatha De Danaan passed from the land, and the descendants of Scota, the legendary Gallic Queen who took the island to create a kingdom for her sons, became the current residents of Ireland. Some believe that the Sidhe made a deal with Queen Scota and her people to take the island for her in exchange for being allowed to live there in peace and solitude because, apparently, the Sidhe remained in Ireland long after the Tuatha De Danaan disappeared. Later era legends describe the Sidhe as a tall, powerful, and beautiful people. Their fair skin eventually earned them the name *fairies*, and they were most often seen strolling along the beach or dancing in forest clearings at twilight.

An encounter with one of these gorgeous and seductive people always promised to be memorable. All who reported meeting them claim to have had similar experiences. A traveler finds himself alone in the woods or at the edge of the beach when he notices the most beautiful person he has ever seen off in the distance, in no particular hurry to be anywhere and usually wearing green—a color so associated with the Sidhe that it was long considered dangerous to wear lest it be an incorrect shade of green and thus offend the Sidhe. The Sidhe, when they notice they are being watched, often shy away, disappearing without a trace. A few approach, though, beginning a seduction that will leave the human alive but, upon waking up the next morning, deeply drained of energy and perhaps nursing a few well-bled cuts. Some stories claim that the human recalled the seduction and subsequent sensual bleeding process by Sidhe, but many more claim that the human blacked out during a frightening draining of his or her life's essence.

Nephilim

In Genesis 6, the Christian Bible mentions a race born of the copulation of angels and human women. According to the Bible, the angels chose the most beautiful of human women to have children by, and those children were giants among men—tall, attractive, intelligent, and strong. The King James version of the book says that "these were the great ones of old, men of renown." But Genesis 6 also seems to suggest that these were not good and kind people, but predators of humanity. The book suggests that their every thought was evil, and chapter 13 of the book of Numbers suggests that wherever these people—the Nephilim—lived, humans were devoured.

It is no wonder that this race is so often characterized as villainous, since these people were actually the deities of much older religions. The term *Nephilim* comes from the Sumerian root *Nfl*, which was another name for their gods, the Annunaki. An, the sky god, and Ki, the earth goddess—the progenitors of the Annunaki—were said to have been created by the joining of a human woman and a powerful spirit being. This oddity of birth was supposed to explain why these two deities and their descendants possessed such great intelligence, wisdom, and spiritual powers.

The Annunaki were teachers and healers, and they were thought to be the earliest rulers of Sumer and Akkad—the heroes of all Babylonian tales. Each member of this race carried the combined symbol of the sun circle (representing An) and the flat line of the horizon (Ki) as a charm on a necklace or a large symbol carried in the hand for ceremonial purposes (such as in the surviving stone carvings of the creature thought to be Lilith). In this symbol, the sun circle sits atop the flat horizon line—an image of sunset or sunrise, and a perfect representation of the twilight nature of what the Hebrew and Christian peoples would later call the Nephilim, a people that likely both led humanity and fed on it.

In fact, many of the descendants of An and Ki—such as the Ekimmu, the Uruku, and the Seven Demons—are reported in Babylonian mythology as needing to feed upon human blood or energy to nourish themselves. The most famous of all these divine descendants, though, is Lilith.

Modern fiction, including the comic book *Crimson*, is fond of portraying Lilith as the mother of all vampires—the first of her kind and the progenitor of the race. Hebrew mythologies describe her as Adam's first wife, rejected due to a lack of submissiveness; in revenge for her rejection, she swore a curse upon Adam and all his descendants, damning herself to giving birth to a race of half demons who would prey upon all of humanity. However, the original story of Lilith suggests that she was a lesser child of An and Ki, and relatively insignificant. She played a minor role in the hero epic of Gilgamesh, being nothing more than a harmful spirit taking up residence in a tree.

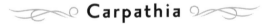

Carpathia

The real Dracula was not the first of the vampires nor was he the origin of vampire myths. In fact, Vlad Dracula grew up in a beautiful land rich with vampiric folklore, and he likely used that folklore intentionally to encourage the myths that surrounded him. The peoples of the region of eastern Europe near the Carpathian Mountains are known for their folktales, the most famous of which are about vampires—creatures that they call the *Strigoi*.

The *Strigoi Morte* are the vampiric spirits who roam and hunt without bodies, feeding on the energies of living humans, sometimes when the humans are sleeping or dreaming, and sometimes while they are wide awake and simply in the wrong place at the wrong time. Unlike the vampires of modern legends, the Strigoi Morte are not considered demons or the angry spirits of those who were murdered or not buried properly. The people of this region, even today, simply believe that the Strigoi Morte are the spirits of *Strigoi Vii*—living vampires—and are no longer in possession of a physical body.

The Strigoi Vii, sometimes also called *Moroii*, are thought to be a race similar to humanity but different in their need to feed on human energy or human blood. Although there are thought to be other types of vampires in the region, they are the most well known, particularly among the Gypsies who live there.

The Gypsies—or *Roma*, the term some prefer—remain an often nomadic people, spread through many countries, but with a long history in Romania in

particular. They have a great love of fantastical stories and scary tales, but behind each of their fictions is a backbone of facts—even their stories of vampires. According to them, the Strigoi Vii were a tall, beautiful, pale, strong, intelligent, well-mannered, regal, and often wealthy people— usually landowners, businessmen, and, historically, even royalty and nobility.

Like the Strigoi Morte, the Strigoi Vii primarily fed upon the life energies of humanity, picking a single volunteer to feed from for a length of time. According to the Gypsies, the Strigoi Vii could also feed on human blood, but it was only the young and inexperienced who chose to do so. Much as was suggested in Bram Stoker's novel *Dracula*, the Gypsies and vampires in this region, especially in Romania, have a long history of working together amicably. The wealthy, landowning Strigoi Vii could provide the Gypsy caravans with fair pay for manual labor or entertainment, as well as safe passage through their land, in particular protecting the Gypsy people from discrimination and potential attackers. The Roma would also provide one valuable service that the discreet vampires of the region could not do without: food.

The Gypsies and vampires of the region practiced a tradition they referred to as *lording*, whereby one Gypsy, usually a female volunteer, would be chosen to go live with the Strigoi for the time her family was on the land. The vampire was generally allowed to feed upon her at his leisure, and her family was protected in return. And though it was not an actual part of the bargain, the vampire would always treat the guest with the utmost respect and often bring gifts to the family as a show of traditional vampiric gratitude. According to members of the Carbone de Travois Gypsy family, this arrangement was still in common practice not even eighty years ago in Romanian lands. One member of that family professes that her great-aunt Piranda was lorded out to a wealthy vampire in the 1910s and '20s.

Piranda's younger sister Nia described the vampire as very tall with light brown hair, always immaculately dressed, and perfectly clean shaven, with a lithe, masculine physique. Nia added that he smelled "pretty." In 1918, when Piranda spent the summer with him, he had the first car Nia had ever seen. Among other things, he gave the family oxen and cows, blankets, clothes of all kinds, and permission to cut his trees and hunt the wild game on his land. Nia said he seemed to genuinely care about Piranda, inviting her back to his home every summer when the family passed through, going so far as to keep a special campground cleared for them, with a well that only they were allowed to use.

Nia said her sister returned to the family at the end of each summer looking "fit and fine like old wine."

Piranda's vampire, whose name has been lost to time, is far from the only Strigoi Vii to have been reported in the area. Most everyone has heard of Prince Vlad Dracula, "the Impaler." Born in Transylvania in 1431, he ruled Romania during a difficult time. The Turks were attacking in waves, and with his forces completely outnumbered, he used his intelligence to wage psychological warfare on his enemies, which also served to keep his own people in line and instilled confidence that they would prevail. As long as he lived, he kept peace in his land and kept the enemies on the run. However, not so many people know about this famous vampire's brethren, or even about his master.

Prince Vlad Dracula was the son of Vlad Dracul, "the Dragon," and his name literally meant "Vlad, son of the Dragon." Both he and his father were members of the Ordo Dracul, the Order of the Dragon—an organization made up of eastern Europe royalty. Surviving Gypsy families claim that, throughout the history of this region, most of the nobility were Strigoi Vii, which lends some credence to the claims some make that the membership of the order was exclusive to vampires, the term *dragon* being used as a code word for *vampire*. Oddly, this fact was most likely well known at the time, since Christians of the period,

particularly in that region, would often refer to vampires as devils, demons, or dragons. And in the case of the Romanian language, one word, *dracul*, meant all three of those things at the same time. A case in point: the incubi and succubi of medieval folktales are interchangeably called both "vampires" and "demons."

Prince Vlad not only had underlings among the other vampires; he also had a master. Few stories mention Dracula's lord and master, the king of the region in that day, and it is doubtful that many even wonder about his existence. His name was Matthias Corvinus. Likely a Strigoi Vii himself, King Matthias was far from intimidated by the Impaler. In fact, he once had the prince imprisoned for three years, or possibly longer, due to various political motivations and his need to have a less independent prince in Vlad's position. A wise and peaceful man, Corvinus was far from the warlord he is claimed to have been in the popular cinematic depictions of the underworld, finally committing his armies to the defense of Romania only after Vlad had fallen in love with and requested the hand of a relative of his, likely the sister of the king—Vlad's request, incidentally, having been made during his captivity in the king's castle.

The Strigoi Vii type of vampire certainly has a deep history in the region of the Carpathian Mountains, documented by writers such as the monk Montague Summers and recounted in the stories of Gypsy families like the Carbone de Travois band. It is probably because of this history that modern vampires often use the term *Strigoi Vii* when describing themselves, especially when trying to avoid the stigma that often accompanies the term *vampire*.

Other Cultures

Much like the vampires that Buffy slays, the "vampires" of the Korowai people of Papua New Guinea are thought to be demonic spirits who have taken up residence in a human body. Known as *khakhua*, or "witch-men," these men—for it is only the men that can be possessed—are thought to be monsters from the world of the supernatural who have taken over human bodies by vampirically consuming and replacing their spirits. Once it has done so, a *khakhua* proceeds to kill the human's closest relatives by attacking them in their sleep, consuming their organs and replacing them with fire ash, and eventually finishing the victim off by shooting a magical arrow into her heart. Like the vampires of other cultures, the *khakhua* are thought to spread disease and discomfort in those around them.

The Korowai believe that the only way to defeat these vampiric spirits is to hunt them down, fill them full of arrows, and eat the flesh they inhabit. Children are generally kept away from these cannibal feasts because they are particularly susceptible to the evil spirits that are freed there. For the sake of decency, children who are accused of being *khakhua* are allowed to age to adulthood before they are turned into a tribal feast.

Similar to the organ-consuming *khakhua* of Papua New Guinea are the ghouls of Arabia. Considered to be a type of djinn, ghouls are thought to be half human and half demon and generally to feed on the flesh of the freshly dead, though they are occasionally known to lure travelers to remote ruins, where they attack them and suck their blood. But ghouls are not the only djinns with vampiric tendencies. In fact djinns, often known in the West as *genies*, get their reputation for granting wishes from the idea that they could use their immense powers to help or serve humans in exchange for the chance to slowly siphon energy from their souls.

In Chinese myth, the Ch'ing Shih is thought to be a demon who has taken possession of a dead body, thereby preserving it from decay. Described as having red eyes, sharp talons, piranhalike teeth, and a body covered in white hair, the Ch'ing Shih were thought to prey upon other corpses or upon the living, draining blood from their victims and even removing their heads. In some cases, these beings are even said to be able to fly through the air at great speed. Burning the bodies of these creatures to ash, it seems, is the only reliable way to put their wicked spirits to rest.

Also in the Asian region was the Penanggalan. This Malaysian vampire is described as a floating human head with the stomach still attached. It flew about at night seeking the blood of its favored prey, newborn infants. The tale of the Penanggalan's creation tells of a woman who somehow managed to behead herself during a religious ceremony for penance.

The *bajang* and *langsuir* were also from Malaysia. Both belong to the same species of demon-vampire, the *bajang* being the male and the *langsuir*, the female. They are said to have operated in the same capacity as a witch's familiar, assisting magic users in learning the dark arts, being passed along through family lines, and serving their owners in any way they see fit. These creatures were supposed to be quite beautiful, with long nails and hair, usually wearing fine robes of green cloth. The females were supposed to be considerably more dangerous and aggressive than the males, but easily tamable if one could manage to cut the *langsuir's* hair and nails quite short and stuff the stolen locks into the hole in the back of her neck, the orifice that she would use to suck the blood of her infant victims. Once tamed, these creatures were supposed to have made fine spouses and lovers and are said to have been unmatched in their child-rearing talents.

The Ashanti people of central Ghana, in West Africa, also have a number of interesting beliefs about vampires. The *asasabonsam*, for instance, is supposed to be a creature of human shape that lives deep in the forests and is only occasionally encountered by hunters. Those who do encounter an *asasabonsam* rarely survive, for it sits in the treetops, awaiting passing prey which it snatches up with the hooks it has instead of feet. These hooks are attached to the ends of long legs, which dangle all the way to the ground. An *asasabonsam* consumes its prey with its metal teeth, and the creature may be somewhat family oriented, given the reported sightings of groups of male, female, and child *asasabonsam*.

The Ashanti also believe in a vampire called the *obayifo*, a humanoid creature that prefers to suck the blood of children. The *obayifo* leave their bodies at night to seek prey or cast curses upon crops. In this disembodied state they are said to emit a phosphorescent light, though in their everyday lives the only signs that they might be abnormal are their sharp, shifty eyes, which seem never to be at rest, as well as their abnormally persistent appetites, which generally lead to an obsession with food.

When many of these African peoples were forcibly transported to the New World, so, too were many of their beliefs. This was particularly true for the small country of Grenada, where the *loogaroo* are said to dwell. These creatures are said to be human beings, particularly old women, who have made a pact with the devil or with one of the demons particular to the native religion. The devil or demon grants the human certain magical powers in exchange for fresh warm blood each night. So, each night the *loogaroo* makes her way to a silk-cotton tree, where she sheds her skin, folding it neatly and hiding it nearby, and takes flight in the shape of a sulfurous ball of blue flame. Barred doors and locked windows do nothing to stop *loogaroo*, who are known to be able to slip through even the tiniest crack. They are said to be susceptible to physical attack, however, receiving cuts or wounds in their flesh if in their flame form they are stabbed or sliced with a blade.

The native peoples of Mexico also have a long history of vampiric mythology. Most of the ancient Mexican deities were vampiric in nature, demanding human sacrifices, still-beating hearts, and gallons upon gallons of blood as offerings. There were also a number of lesser vampiric creatures such as the *ciuapipiltin*—a word meaning "princess"—who was a kind of vampire-witch that dwelt at crossroads and was fond of draining the life energies of children. A *ciuapipiltin* was created when a woman died during the birth of her first child, forever doomed to vent her rage upon all she encountered.

It was also generally believed in ancient Mexico that all magic users and sorcerers were vampiric in nature, sucking the blood of other humans to empower their spells. They were sometimes known to practice this vampirism after having taken the shape of a coyote. It is unclear whether native priests were considered to be among these sorcerer-vampires, but it seems that all such priests were classed as witches by the later invading Spanish army.

In modern Mexico, most of these beliefs have devolved into tabloid headlines about goat-killing creatures. The *chupacabra*, a creature reported to have been seen by hundreds in modern Mexico, is most known for attacking and draining the blood from goats, though it is occasionally said to attack humans as well. It is said to have large, black, oval eyes, or beady little orbs. Witnesses have said its skin was green, brown, black, or even purple and have claimed it to be furry, bald, or scaly. Descriptions vary from a two-legged mammal to a quadrupedal reptile or even a winged creature with feathered or leathery wings.

CHAPTER 2

Modern Vampires

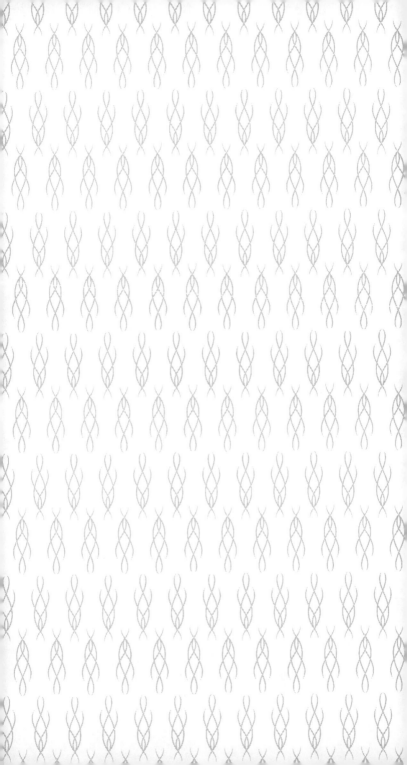

Fictions and folktales about blood-sucking or energy-draining beings have entertained and frightened humanity for millennia. But like all stories, these tales may contain a deeper truth. Certainly myths of dangerous creatures roaming the streets and forests after dark were used to warn children away from places frequented by robbers, murderers, and other predators, but the common features of these stories from vastly different lands, time periods, and cultures cannot be ignored. What are the ties that connect these tales?

If there is an answer, it may lie within the so-called modern vampires, a race of humanity that hails from many different backgrounds but whose members all have the same assertion: that they are more than human. They believe that their flesh is basically human in form and function, but that their minds and spirits are distinctly different. Human yet inhuman, these creatures identify most closely with the stories of the mythical and historical vampires. Often calling themselves *Strigoi Vii* or *vampyres*, these people seem to have much in common with the ancient myths and often profess to be the very creatures these myths were based upon. There is no telling how old this race truly is, but there seems to be some validity to the claims.

The Vampiric Child

Nearly every vampire alive today was born to human parents. Most begin their lives in the same ways as

any other person. Some are born rich, some poor, some healthy, some sick, but often they are gifted with high intelligence. As the vampire matures, differences between him and the humans surrounding him quickly begin to emerge. Young vampires eagerly consume information, learning all they can, examining how things operate, and observing the behavior of those around them. It is in these early years that young vampires usually begin to first realize that they may be different in some way from others, even others of comparable intelligence. It is also in these early years that many young vampires turn their minds toward less common intellectual pursuits. Whether influenced by unrealized memories from past lives or simply by the craving to feed their growing minds, young vampires will quickly turn to educating themselves about ancient civilizations, foreign cultures, old religions, and mysticism of every kind.

As with any other child, the young vampire's growing body, with its high metabolism, is primarily designed to fuel the growing intelligence, both in the flesh of the brain and in the strength of the mind. In fact, the average adult human body devotes 20 percent of its resources to fueling the brain. In young vampires, the majority of the body's intake is burned up by the brain. Some vampiric children even begin overeating in an attempt to compensate for this drain on the body. In earlier times, this behavior led to the Celtic folktales regarding changelings—young children who supposedly could eat a family out of house and home and yet never have their appetites sated. The theory at the time was that such children, while still looking like their human parents, had to be Sidhe, or *fairies*, switched with a human child at the child's birth.

Though there are many explanations as to why vampires are part of our consciousness, there is one undeniable fact about these creatures: vampires have a greater need for energy than do other humans. Eventually, the energetic needs of the young vampire's spirit outstrip the ability of her body to keep up with them. For many vampires, this strain on the body results in a sickly childhood, and sometimes severe depression. The strain on the body often reaches culmination in the teen years, when the vampire's metabolism starts to slow and other changes begin. The powerful vampire spirit has begun to starve.

The Hunger

As the spirit begins to starve, a vampire gets his first taste of what it truly is to know the Hunger. At first, it feels like any other craving for sustenance. Like a deep want of food or water, this ravenous need comes on slowly and builds in strength over several years. As in his childhood, the young vampire will attempt to eat and drink to fill the need, but nothing will help. As the cult classic movie *The Hunger* made clear, no human food can relieve this need.

Instinctively, the vampire will begin to seek high-energy situations. Arguments with friends or family members, difficult and often stressful relationships, and even unhealthy group environments all become arenas for the vampire's early, unconscious attempts to feed. At this point, the young vampire will still be far from truly understanding why these difficult settings may partially sate his deep need, even bringing on a sense of calm amid the distress and chaos. But on some level his conscious mind will already be opening up to the possibility that he may somehow be very different from those around him, that there may be something fundamentally puzzling within him.

Searching for an answer to the Hunger, many young vampires will seek the help of medical practitioners, only to be eventually turned away, conventional tests and knowledge having revealed absolutely nothing. Many more will seek out metaphysical writings or prowl through the Internet for answers to the half-formed questions rising in the backs of their minds. It becomes a search for the self and for community, driven forward by a subtle feeling that the vampire needs to know something important about himself and, perhaps more important, whether he is alone.

Eventually, answers are found. Whether from a book, from a computer screen, or even from the lips of another, these answers often come in the form of terms like *the Hunger* and *Human Living Vampire*,—which provide both understanding and the comfort of knowing that others have been through this before. This simple revelation begins a process of deeper understanding and a reevaluation of previous mind-sets and philosophies—a process that since ancient times has been known as *the Awakening*.

The Awakening

The first recorded use of the vampiric term *Awakening* is in the epic Celtic tale of the Second Battle of Mag Tuired. In line eighty-three of the tale, as translated by Elizabeth A. Gray, Lug, the hero of the Tuatha De Danaan, an unbeatable champion sired by a Fomoire king, is instructed by the goddess Morrigan to "awake." The remainder of the passage, the part that most likely explained how

Lug was to awaken his Sidhe nature and talents so that he could win the upcoming battle, was supposedly untranslatable.

There are many forms of Awakening, and all mean relatively the same thing: opening one's mind to the wider reality, often to the reality of energy and the spiritual world. For human magickal practitioners, an Awakening occurs when they first realize that their desires can be focused to create change in the world around them; for the psychically gifted, an Awakening occurs when they open themselves to the concept that the things they see and hear in their minds may be not only real, but very useful in their daily lives; and for a vampire, an Awakening is the realization that she is, in fact, undeniably a vampire. Awakening begins when a vampire first considers that she might not be entirely human. It continues as she learns what she is and finally fully accepts it. The process never truly ends. A vampire is always learning about what she is, because her survival depends on her continued education into what she is, what she needs, and what she can do.

An Awakening can be traumatic for the young vampire. In many cases the vampire has had little or no personal experience with the supernatural and esoteric and is forced to completely rethink how he sees the world. And even those who have a background in the metaphysical or even a family history of witchcraft or other mystical traditions have rarely been exposed to the honest truth about vampires. So, suddenly much of what the young vampire has been taught in his life is turned upside down and questioned. This process usually occurs during the teen years, when much in a person's life is already being reevaluated and examined. The concept that someone may not be fully hu-

man seems a bit more comprehensible at that age, since adult mind-set has yet to be deeply ingrained and the childlike wonderment about the world has not quite worn off. However, some are not so fortunate.

Awakening for some vampires does not occur in the late teens or early twenties, or in some cases even later. When an Awakening does come for these late bloomers, it is often set off by other disruptions in the person's life: the ending of a long relationship, the empty-nest syndrome, or the loss of a loved one. In this case, the Awakening is finally accepted and possible only because the vampire's reality is already in question. However, the Awakening itself becomes a further disruption, another situation to deal with on top of the rest, and one that may send the person over the edge, forcing her to seek professional help. Most vampires are strong enough to handle the Awakening no matter when it comes, and all are happier once they accept it and become more complete persons, not unlike Anne Rice's character Louis when he finally accepted his true nature.

On the opposite end of the spectrum are those extremely rare individuals who are born Awakened or Awaken at a very early age, long before puberty. Known as *Dhampyri*, from a very early age, these creatures have a solid understanding of what they are, what they need, and how to get it, though this does not change the fact that they are children and have to live with the fear that speaking of strange things to their often close-minded parents will result in a long stay among white-coated men with nets. The stress and loneliness of such a condition will cause most Dhampyri to block out the understanding of what they are, selectively ignoring parts of that knowledge until a bit later in life so that their minds do not become overwhelmed by the greater reality that all Awakened vampires have no choice but to see. Rarer still are those Dhampyri who choose to face and own what they are at an early age and so must constantly deal with the Hunger and its effect on their young lives. They must deal with parents, friends, and school counselors who constantly question their sanity and behavior, even when they do not reveal their secret.

Some believe that the Dhampyri are the oldest of vampiric spirits, that the knowledge of their vampiric nature has been collected and reaffirmed so many times over so many lives that it simply impresses itself upon the brain of the child without effort. This belief is supported by the fact that Dhampyri often display greater abilities, a stronger Hunger, and even higher intelligence than other vampires, all of which are thought to be a product of the natural growth and development a spirit achieves with time and determination.

The Modern Vampire Community

The basic purpose behind the formation of any community is to provide a safe environment where people can gather for the purposes of learning about themselves and their needs, and where those who have recently realized that they are part of the community can see that they are not alone. The modern vampire community has five primary functions:

1. Helping the newly Awakened
2. Guidance and education
3. Research
4. The dissemination of information
5. Organization

To help the newly Awakened, the vampire community has effectively created a kind of outreach program. They have done this by publishing a number of books, such as *The Psychic Vampire Codex* and *The Ethical Psychic Vampire*, that explain the basic concepts of modern vampires, their community, and their needs, as well as often providing information on how to get in touch with others in the community; and through informational Web pages such as the Drink Deeply and Dream forums (*www.drinkdeeplyanddream.com*), which often simply provide acceptance and basic help for new vampires as well as the occasional legal nugget that a vampire might find handy, such as where laws against blood drinking, blood letting, or even claiming to be a vampire (illegal in Muslim countries) are in force. In addition, it is common for vampires to be drawn to one another via telepathy, unconscious or otherwise. Those who have long been part of the vampire community often provide the support a young vampire needs. This "beacon," the method by which modern vampires psychically recognize their own, will be discussed in more detail later.

Being a young vampire is not easy, and guidance and education are vitally important, especially just after the initial Awakening. The young must be taught how to control their Hunger and to feed responsibly, as well as to control the psychic sensitivities that are common traits of vampires. Young vampires must be encouraged not to shut these sensitivities down in order to avoid dealing with the confusion and anxiety they often bring, as this is not the best or healthiest approach. These natural psychic abilities are a useful tool for finding healthy energy to feed on; therefore, the best approach is to teach the young how to incorporate these gifts into their daily lives and use them both well and ethically.

The vampire community continually provides educational opportunities for vampires of all ages and experience levels. Everyone in the community is encouraged to educate themselves in the metaphysical, but also in the mundane. Vampires with multiple college degrees are highly respected, partially for their ability to approach the research of vampire kind from an educated, scientific perspective.

Scientific research on vampires is becoming more important as the community grows and its members

demand a deeper understanding of the facts behind their existence. Some of the larger organizations, such as the Atlanta Vampire Alliance, have developed the resources to do large-scale research. This organization has invested massive amounts of time and effort in conducting statistical surveys of those who identify as vampires in an attempt to gain an understanding of vampires' common medical conditions. House Kheperu has done extensive work on applying the scientific method to the exploration of the psychological and spiritual side of the vampire nature.

The dissemination of information has also become an important responsibility of the community and its leaders. Real vampires are still a scary topic for many people, so as the vampire community has grown and become more public, it has become important for the community to develop a healthy public image.

People like the author and community leader Michelle Belanger use their talents as public speakers to discuss modern vampires both in college halls and on television and radio. Don Henry, famous for being a part of the reality experiment *Mad Mad House* on the Sci Fi Channel, has opened his life up to the cameras, allowing a general audience to see that, as a vampire, he may be eccentric, but he is far from criminal or dangerous.

The final task of the vampire community is to provide a level of organization for the vampiric world. While the vast majority of vampires do not officially belong to any organized group, some do. Often called *houses* or *orders*, these groups provide a familial atmosphere for those who are attracted to their hierarchical structures. They also help give a sense of order and unity to the vampire public at large, often providing the community with guidance as it grows, and supplying sensible rules of ethics and etiquette, such as the Black Veil, a set of thirteen rules laid down by Father Sebastian of House Sahjaza in 1997 to define how a vampire should behave in public, private, and especially amongst other vampires.

Most of the vampire houses are young, formed in the last ten to twenty years, but a few can rightfully claim a lineage much older than that, having originally formed directly from the traditions of ancient vampiric families such as the Order of the Dragon, the one Prince Vlad's family belonged to, or the many Sidhe families of Ireland. In essence, these groups are the

community's government, providing order, structure, and even arbitration when needed, existing only to serve the community, and surviving solely through the support of the community.

CHAPTER 3

Basics of
Vampiric Feeding

Feeding Tendrils

In many ways, spirits operate in much the same ways as single-cell organisms. There is an outer protective membrane, the physical body, and several inner core structures, the chakras, that have certain functions to perform. Most spirits cannot steal resources— energy—from an outside source unless there is direct membrane contact together with a significant interior lack of that resource. Vampires, however, have developed a way of manipulating their exterior environment so that they can feed without the need to be close to the source. Thus, the use of their feeding tendrils, the writhing masses that make up their outermost layers.

These tendrils, which are made of the same electromagnetic energies that all spirits are made of, have evolved primarily for the purpose of feeding from other spirits. They are denser and more refined than the more basic energies of human spirits, not unlike how a bodybuilder's muscles are denser and more developed than the average person's. Given their adaptability and elasticity, the tendrils allow vampires to connect with and feed from spirits not in their immediate proximity.

Tesla's Wireless Electricity

A renowned scientist and contemporary of both Albert Einstein and Thomas Alva Edison, Nikola Tesla originally came to America in 1884 to work at Edison Machine Works. It was not long before he found his way out from under Edison's shadow and made his own mark on the scientific world with various inventions, including alternating current. Beyond his inventions, Tesla also made his mark with many theories that were far beyond his time. In particular, his theory of wireless electricity not only evidences Tesla's instinctive understanding of electromagnetism but has become the basis for a scientific understanding of the principles behind vampiric feeding.

Tesla's theory of wireless energy transfer is both elegant and simple. The basic concept is that when two

waves of the same frequency—for example, electromagnetic waves—contact one another, the waves cancel
each another out, leaving only the energy that was
contained within the waves—in this case, electrons. If
the two waves are broadcast at the same amplitude, the
energy is simply dispersed outward into the environment. But if one of the waves is of lower amplitude, an
interesting thing happens: the energy begins to flow toward the source of the wave with the lower amplitude,
allowing it to be collected and used by that source. Like
water flowing through a pipe, the energy follows the
path of least resistance. In nature, the lower-amplitude
wave will most commonly absorb the new energy and
use it to increase its own amplitude until the power
levels of the two waves are equal. When the reaction is
controlled by an intelligence, however, the energy can
be channeled elsewhere—for
example, into a battery, an appli-
ance, or a separate electromagnetic wave.

Thus electricity can be transferred from one place to another
without the use of wires, though
this transfer is impractical for
daily use. If a modern-day power
company were to attempt to use
a wireless system to get power
to its customers, it would run
into the same problems the local

water company has. The usage of meters to determine how much to charge customers would become necessary; service to the more outlying customers would be poor; and, though the removal of unsightly power poles would improve the look of most neighborhoods and reduce the likelihood of power outages, some power would be lost as it escapes earth's atmosphere or could be stolen by energy thieves using unregistered antennas. Essentially, the major problems with Tesla's system lie in the inability of modern science to focus the energy transfer.

Nikola Tesla's theory is invaluable in understanding how vampires feed. Vampires are able to capitalize on a free source of energy: the energy that human spirits constantly radiate, flooding the world around them.

The Hunt

Once a vampire has made a conscious decision to feed, she must select her target: a proper human to feed from. This process of selection and seduction is sometimes called the *hunt*, and the target is often called the *prey*—a term that is in no way intended to be derogatory, just straightforward. The White Court vampires of Jim Butcher's *Dresden Files* novels have an amusingly similar approach.

Vampires begin the hunt with prey selection. A wise vampire will always choose a candidate from afar, preferring to take his pick from the drove of strangers who pass through his usual hangouts rather than from his own circle of friends, relatives, or work associates. Should anything go bad with the feeding process, it is important that the vampire be able to put significant distance between himself and the selected prey. Many deeper feeding methods, discussed in the next chapter, require the cooperation of the prey, which usually means the prey will have to know that the vampire is a vampire. If for any reason the prey is tied in some way with the vampire's normal daily work or social life, an accidental slip of the tongue could lead to a very disruptive situation for the vampire.

Each vampire has her own preference for prey. Many younger vampires, with lesser needs, will prefer to feed from crowds, preventing them from having to put any real effort into prey selection, and as long as their energy needs are not great, this method will do them well for many years. But for most vampires, an individual must be selected for the occasional deeper feeding. These people will be selected according to the vampire's tastes, often matching the vampire's own fashion and social preferences and thereby being easily incorporated into the vampire's existing circle of friends, although this is not always the case. In fact, many vampires occasionally prefer to target prey who are either closed minded or inexperienced with the less ordinary side of reality. The extra shock these types of prey go through when their minds are gently opened to a darker reality will cause them to produce larger quantities of energy for a time.

Regardless of the vampire's personal tastes, the prey should be healthy and fit, both physically and psychologically. Any sign of mental or physical weakness will likely turn any vampire off to the idea of feeding from this person, but should instinct fail, logic must step in. A vampire should always take care not to feed from someone who will not be able to handle the process well. Thus no vampire in her right mind would ever feed from anyone who is underage or mentally unstable.

Once a target has been selected, the seduction begins. Every vampire has his own method, but all seductions tend to follow roughly the same pattern. First, the vampire makes initial contact. He finds an excuse to speak to the prey and strike up a conversation, planting the seed of a new friendship. By this time, the vampire will likely already be feeding lightly, tasting the surface energies of the prey.

If all is going well, the vampire may feel comfortable taking the feeding process further. This involves spending plenty of time with the energy source, actively feeding from her and perhaps even starting a relationship with her. Of course, no vampire should ever begin a relationship with any person they do not have a genuine interest in. Romantic relationships can be valuable to the feeding process, but they are far from necessary, and they can be unethical if they are being used only for feeding.

On occasion, some very unwise vampires will take to trying to feed from other vampires. Now, there are many energy-exchange exercises that vampires often engage in with one another, but that is not what is being discussed here. Actively attempting to feed from a vampire, taking energy and returning nothing, is both unethical and potentially dangerous. Vampires young in spirit or body, and the newly Awakened, do not have sufficient training or experience and so are rarely capable of effectively defending themselves against an attack from another vampire. Not only would they be poor sources of nourishment, since they are rarely well fed, but an attack on them would be the equivalent of an attack on the vampire community's children. It is unlikely that attacks of this nature would long go unpunished.

As for attempts by younger vampires to feed from older vampiric spirits, that is a different story entirely. Many have made this mistake, but few have made it more than once. Younger vampires, naturally drawn to and perhaps even fascinated by the massive power reserves within the ancient spirits of some of the eldest, have often allowed themselves to think briefly that such a vampire would either not mind or not notice a small siphoning of his energies. This is not the case. Even the most minor attempt to steal what has been so hard won for these vampires over so many lifetimes does not go unnoticed. In fact, the young rarely have any understanding of the hardships older souls have had to endure—hardships that have turned many of them into secretive and often antisocial creatures. Along with their massive energy reserves comes an equally massive Hunger, one that can be quickly and fiercely turned against anyone reckless enough to attempt to feed from them without permission.

It is for all these reasons that many vampires, when they are finally ready for a deeper and more fulfilling feeding, choose to find a *donor*. A donor is a human who is well informed of both what a vampire is and what a vampire needs. Donors are friends of the vampire community who have made the informed decision to freely donate either their blood, their energy, or both to one or more vampires. Like the lorded-out Gypsies of Romania or even the fictional Dracula's Mina, these people are loved. They are valued friends of the community and are often very well treated by vampires,

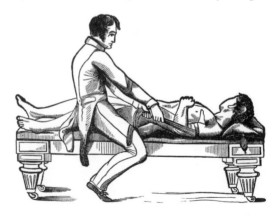

since their cooperation is vital to the deeper feeding process. Most are sworn to secrecy.

The Energy Vacuum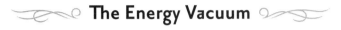

The actual feeding process really is all about the creation of an energy vacuum—a process that all vampires are adept at instinctively, but one that is nevertheless difficult to truly master, since turning it off and on at will can be difficult. It begins when the vampire locks on to the correct frequencies. When a vampire is feeding from another vampire, this process is almost unnecessary, since vampires already have so many frequencies in common. However, feeding from humans is a bit more challenging.

The vampire begins by simply relaxing, letting her tendrils unfurl and reach out to the prey. If the vampire's mind is clear and open, she should immediately feel the difference between the person's energies and her own, sensing how the prey's energies radiate in all directions and, more importantly, how her energies and those of her prey feel incompatible. This incompatibility cannot be forced into abeyance. Instead, as in any bonding experience, it should be allowed to fall away as the vampire focuses her gentle attention on the few commonalities that do exist between the two spirits. Once a common frequency is found, the feeling will be almost instantly noticeable to the vampire as the spiritual energies begin to flow freely between the two.

Most prey will take no notice of this development, but those who are more aware of their energies may take notice, and perhaps even offense, fairly quickly. This is yet another reason that most ethical vampires prefer the use of a donor.

Young vampires feeding for the first time are unlikely to create the link on their first try unless they  are being coached through the process by a more experienced vampire, but as with everything else, practice makes perfect. The more often a vampire practices creating these bonds, the more likely he will be able to create them anytime, anywhere, and with just about anyone.

Once the link is created, the vampire needs to lower the amplitude on his end—that is, lower the energy output to the frequency he is using to forge the temporary bond and create a low-pressure system within his spirit, in much the same way that a closed mouth can create an area of low pressure to draw liquid through a straw. Vampires achieve this by transferring power from the frequencies they share with nonvampires to the electromagnetic waves that are decidedly vampiric. It seems a simple process, but doing it on command is a bit more difficult.

During the feeding process, a young vampire will be quick to allow her psychological state to reflect the aggressive, pushy, and even abusive thought patterns that come so easily when a vampire perceives her prey as nothing more than food. Ethical vampires, no matter how young in spirit or body, move quickly beyond this unmannerly and exploitative frame of mind and into the cold, emotionless state of a true predator.

A detached and emotionless state is best for the feeding process for various reasons. First, emotions of any kind, even aggressive, semipredatory emotions, can cause psychological disturbances that get in the way of the energy transfer. The vampire's attention needs to be fully focused on the prey, not on himself. Second, a colder, more meditative state of mind allows the many other waves that the vampire is simultaneously broadcasting to be smoother, cleaner, and less modulated. Nice, clean waves will often flow through other waves without disrupting them badly, but a distorted and modulated frequency—one caused, in this case, by aggressive thoughts—makes it more likely that the link will be disrupted.

The initial lowering of the amplitude of the linked frequency represents only the first sip taken from the straw. When drinking from a straw, a person's mouth can hold only so much liquid. Once the mouth is full, the liquid must be swallowed to make room for more. The spiritual version of this is almost no different. Once enough energy has been pulled through the link to raise the vampire's end to match the prey's end, the vampire must effectively swallow—that is, she must

transfer the newly gained energy into her other frequencies, in the same way she did when she created the
vacuum in the first place.

Most vampires, particularly when psychically
feeding, will often use breathing techniques to help
facilitate this process physically and psychologically,
taking a long, deep breath in to draw the new energy in,
followed by a full breath out as the energy is transferred
from the linked waves to other waves, where it will
be temporarily stored and later incorporated into the
spirit. Just as with the use of a straw, the energy conduit
is momentarily blocked while the vampire "swallows,"
only to be opened again once a new energy vacuum
is created. This process will be repeated several times
before the vampire is finished feeding and is ready
to break the link. The level of satisfaction ultimately
gained depends on both the vampire's individual needs
and how intimate the bond is between the vampire and
the energy source.

The Weiser Field Guide to Vampires

Though the postfeeding digestion of the energy is almost entirely instinctive, requiring practically no effort on the part of the vampire, it is no less important to the overall process. After feeding, a vampire must take time to relax, time to allow his electromagnetic waves to flow freely and incorporate the new energy evenly throughout the spirit. He can do this by meditating, sleeping, or just taking time to relax. Regardless of the method he chooses, the process cannot be rushed.

What If They Don't Feed

At some point in every vampire's life, she gets around to asking the question, What if I don't feed? Physical injuries, social difficulties, or even highly demanding jobs may create situations that significantly reduce a vampire's opportunities to feed. But it is only when she chooses to experiment with starvation that a vampire can truly answer this question.

The experiment begins when a vampire moves his power into the "human" frequencies, raising their amplitudes and effectively plugging them. The feeding tendrils are then also kept as close to the body as possible to prevent them from stretching out to others and instinctively creating feeding bonds. Other methods of avoiding the feeding process may also be used: avoiding crowds or high-energy atmospheres, rejecting any overly dramatic relationships, and not allowing oneself to get emotional. Unlike Edward's family in the *Twilight* saga, real vampires cannot substitute animals for humans in their feedings.

The Hunger pains will be extreme and will get much worse before they begin to get better. But eventually, just like the physical body, the spirit will get tired of feeling hungry and will then shift into a state of low power usage. Of course, this shift takes only a few hours to occur in the physical body, but it can take a few weeks for the spirit body to experience the same shift. Accepting the fact that sustenance is not coming, the spirit will begin to shut down most of its nonvital functions, conserving what remains of its power for essential uses and emergencies.

This low-power, half-starved state is not unlike the state that older un-Awakened vampires settle into after circumstances or choices conspired to prevent them from Awakening during their teens or early twenties. Once settled into this state, an un-Awakened vampire will likely not get out of it until a significant shock or some other change occurs to disrupt her daily life or sense of reality. Unlike those who engage in the starvation experiments, however, the un-Awakened can remain in a low-power state indefinitely due to the limited amount of sustenance provided to them through unconscious feeding, a process that is voluntarily controlled and restricted in the experimenters.

Much as it was before his Awakening, the vampire's energy reserve will eventually be completely used up.

When this happens, the Hunger will reassert itself much more forcefully than before, causing crippling pain and irrationally aggressive behavior. The vampire's conscious mind, thoroughly weakened from starvation, may lose dominance, allowing the more primitive parts of the brain to take control. What is worse is that this transition—from low-energy, highly controlled vampire to ravenous, out-of-control monster—is more subtle than one can imagine. The Hunger may very well be in control long before the vampire or anyone close to her realizes that it has resurfaced.

In this state, a vampire is likely to do just about anything he must to get what he needs. Aggressive and greedy, a vampire this deeply under the influence of his Hunger may make John Carpenter's fictional vampires seem docile by comparison. He may also find, unfortunately, that feeding is not as easy as it used to be. The energy blocks, mental shields, and other hindrances to the feeding process that the vampire has maintained during this experiment, which will have lasted anywhere from nine months to two years by this point, are not so easy to take down once they have been in place for so long. The spirit's internal movement and operations have become debilitated by the lack of power, and though the loss may be too subtle for most to detect, the vampire may find that some of his frequencies have weakened so far as to be lost permanently. The vampire will most commonly experience this as a permanent loss of memory or even a temporary reduction in intelligence.

The human body is capable of surviving on surprisingly little food and water for extended periods of time once certain natural systems have engaged to protect the body's vital functions, but if it is not fed eventually, the body will inevitably sustain permanent damage. The human spirit, whether vampire or not, is no different.

CHAPTER 4

Psychic Feeding

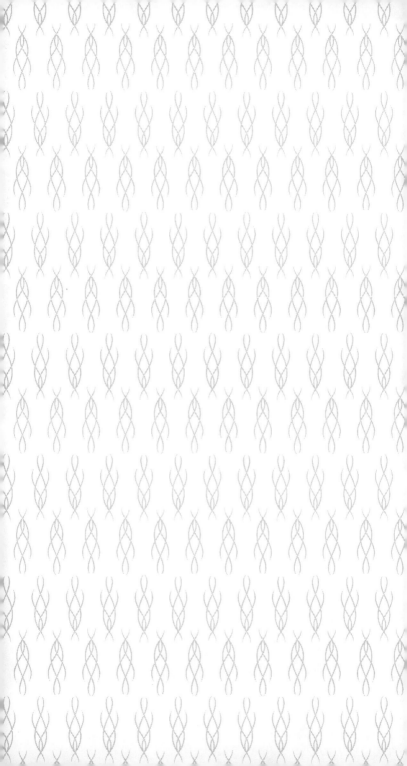

～∞ Conscious ∞～
vs. Unconscious Feeding

Unconscious feeding occurs when a vampire feeds without realizing she is feeding. When a vampire is feeding unconsciously, her spirit acts of its own accord, allowing her tendrils to reach out and take in any excess energy they can reach. Feeding in this manner, without intention, supplies only the bare minimum amount of energy necessary to maintain the basic functioning of the vampiric spirit, and it often causes unhealthy situations. A vampire feeding unconsciously may unintentionally seek out high-energy situations, drama-filled relationships, and even dangerously energetic crowds—all just to temporarily raise her energy to a more comfortable level.

Conscious feeding can occur only after a vampire has begun his Awakening. The act of choosing to feed makes all the difference. Once a vampire is aware of

the energies that surround him, and of his ability to manipulate these energies, he is able to learn much deeper and more satisfying methods of feeding. Awareness is necessary if the vampire ever wants to rise above the bare minimums of basic survival. In fact, when consciously feeding, a vampire does not necessarily have to be terribly hungry. He can feed when he chooses to do so, taking extra energy when it is available, allowing himself the luxury of always keeping a store of energy stashed away should times become less than abundant.

Psychic feeding, or *psy-feeding,* is the most basic and primary way in which all vampires feed. Even blood feeders and un-Awakened vampires psychically feed to a certain extent, usually unconsciously. Psychic feeling involves a direct transfer of energy from one spirit to another via the conduit created by a vampire's feeding tendrils. It was the first method by which vampires took the life from others, and it still remains the most common, though there are many ways of doing it. Each method of psy-feeding has its own level of intensity and exists as a step on the path toward an ever-increasing level of intimacy.

Ambient Feeding

Ambient feeding occurs when a person with lower amplitude inhabits a room together with people of greater amplitude. Without even trying, the lower-amplitude person begins to absorb the power surrounding him. Effectively, the energy simply flows downhill until the lesser electromagnetic field rises to match those surrounding it.

Often, this form of feeding happens unconsciously. Un-Awakened vampires feed like this almost constantly, though Awakened vampires usually keep this process under control when it is not needed. This form of feeding transfers so little energy and requires so little effort on the feeder's part that even human spirits feed in this way from time to time. Of course, they do not have tendrils stretching out into their surroundings to draw the energy in, but a very weak human spirit will naturally suck up any energy it comes into contact with. This is why it is so important that those who are hospitalized have visitors: they need their rooms to be filled with the energy that their bodies may be too sick to produce on

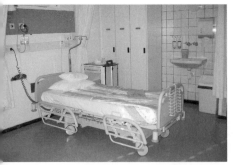

their own. Ironically, this also explains why some psychically sensitive people fear hospitals: they can feel the diseased drawing energy from them.

Surface Feeding

Surface feeding is one step up on the intimacy level of psychic feeding. Surface feeding occurs when a vampire extends her tendrils inside the aura and outer edges of another person's spirit. Essentially, she is licking the person, lapping up the excess energies coming off the person's soul—energies that would normally be lost into the environment.

Most Awakened vampires feed in this way weekly, daily, or however often they may require it. Some even have a need so great that they need to surface-feed two or three times per day just to hold their Hunger at bay.

Strangely enough, since the natural design and instincts of the feeding tendrils cause them to gravitate toward power sources, like roots seeking water, many un-Awakened vampires also feed in this way from time to time. Of course, without directed intent, the feeding is for the most part incidental. The primary difference between ambient and surface feeding is proximity.

Though the shape, size, and number of feeding tendrils vary from vampire to vampire, one fact remains: each vampiric spirit has limits to how far he can safely stretch them. If another spirit is within reach, that spirit will likely be targeted for surface feeding. If not, the vampire will have to stick to ambient feeding.

Conversational Feeding

Simply having a conversation with a vampire can initiate a relatively intimate feeding process, the next step up from surface feeding. In conversational feeding, a back-and-forth communication creates a weak sympathetic bond, tuning both spirits to the same frequency, or to a frequency similar enough to be usable, thereby allowing a cleaner path for energy flow. Usually an Awakened vampire will try to occupy the receptive side of the conversation so that she can encourage the speaker to raise his amplitudes as the conversation deepens. In this way the vampire can focus her attention on adjusting her own waves to be more sympathetically in synch with the speaker's, while she simultaneously lowers her own amplitudes to pull in all the excess energy the speaker is expelling. During conversational feeding, the tendrils do not pass beyond the outer layers of the spirit, but the energy exchange is nonetheless much more intense and satisfying.

Eye contact can help to facilitate conversational feeding by allowing a deeper psychic bond between the conversational partners as they naturally sympathize with one another, but it is not necessary. In fact, conversational feeding can happen even over the phone. It is significantly less effective, but if two are tuned well enough to the same frequencies, electron transfer via the far-traveling extremely low frequencies can occur even if the participants are on different sides of the planet. However, it should be kept in mind that only great empathy can bypass the need to use the feeding tendrils. It also helps that telephones, whether they be land line or cellular, are an electric medium that can be utilized as a possible transfer medium.

While the levels of feeding described previously have little noticeable effect on the person being fed upon, conversational feeding has a clear and noticeable effect, without the need for prolonged exposure. After only a few minutes of this kind of feeding, the average human will begin to feel a little tired and sleepy. A gifted vampire will push the human through this, encouraging him to submerge himself deeper in the intensifying discussion, involving him more personally and emotionally in it, as emotions and strong opinions tend to raise the level of energy expenditure. Once the human has spent all the energy he can spare, the conversation will naturally peter out. A few minutes later, the human will begin to feel the full effects of the drain. Most seek rest immediately and tend to sleep deeply until the energy is replenished.

Simple Touch Feeding

The simple touch intimacy level of psychic feeding is initiated by any physical contact, whether it is as brief and impersonal as a handshake or a pat on the back, or as friendly as a hug or a kiss on the cheek. Even a fingertip lightly pressed against an elbow will do.

As the denser portions of the spirit of each individual, the portions that extend only to just outside the skin, come into contact, a feeding tendril can easily be inserted deep into the human's spirit. The nerve endings in any part of the skin can be used as a conduit to connect the tendrils to the core nervous system and therefore to any part of the human's energy body, but coming into contact with an area that is already close to a power center—a chakra—makes the entire process easier and more efficient. A very hungry vampire could probably drop a human to his knees with a handshake, but the average vampire needs to touch somewhere close to the heart or throat to get anywhere near that kind of reaction. Either way, direct chakra feeding should not be attempted until the vampire has a well-developed knowledge of his Hunger.

Unfortunately, simple touch feeding is not quite as easy to achieve as it sounds. Many humans, even those who are far from Awakened, have a natural ability to sense the predator within. Because of this, they often instinctively withdraw from the vampire's touch, pulling back like an animal that smells danger.

Some humans are actually attracted to the Hunger, drawn in by its want and their own need to be relieved of the tensions they harbor. For these people, the most effective simple touch feeding method is massage.

Having a natural ability to both sense and relieve energy buildups and blockages, vampires often make excellent masseurs and masseuses. Vampires can effectively "see" the muscles lying beneath the skin, how their energies flow, and specifically where tension is causing them to flow incorrectly. It should be constantly kept in mind, though, that at this intimacy level, the massage should be kept light and friendly.

Donor Feeding

Every once in a while, a vampire is lucky enough to encounter a donor—a human who is truly willing to give of her energies to feed the vampire. These are the kinds of people Romanian vampires sought for their lording practice. The openness and knowledge of donors and their willingness to involve themselves in the feeding process allows a higher level of intimacy, and the vampire is able to feed even more deeply than before.

Other than the human's awareness of being fed upon, there is no difference between donor feeding and simple touch feeding. The same physical actions and energetic manipulations occur, the difference being that everyone involved knows the truth. Trust is key, and trust is why no vampire would ethically move on to the next intimacy level without fully informing her partner of the situation and its possible risks.

Intimate Touch

Intimate touch is any physical contact of a sexual or romantic nature short of actual sexual penetration. The contact can be as light and friendly as a kiss on the lips or as sexual as intense foreplay or even full orgasm. Clearly, the point of this deeply intimate form of feeding is to pull the donor out of her distracting surroundings through intense physical stimulation, while also raising her energies to the highest possible amplitude. A strong, focused orgasm has an energy quality that few other things can match, but it is important to note that casual sexual contact does not have nearly the same strength as the energies that emanate from a place of love.

Alternatively, intimate touch does not have to be purely sexual or even pleasurable in nature. The simple bond forged between a professional tattoo artist or piercer and a customer can be used for intimate-touch feeding due to the natural intensity of the body-modification process.

Intercourse

As with any relationship, the step following deep intimacy is full, penetrative intercourse. Psychically feeding during sex is significantly more fulfilling than the typically one-sided intimate touch-feeding level, since the vampire immerses herself into the act, lessening her psychic shields and the constant control she has over her Hunger. Deep, loving, intense sex allows both the donor and the vampire to simply indulge in the feeding process without distraction.

Since this is the lowest intimacy level in which a vampire voluntarily releases some of his control of the Hunger, it is the first level that has the potential to become truly dangerous for the donor. Of course, there are younger spirits who engage in intercourse feeding quite often and simply are not strong enough to be a danger. There are also older vampires who have a Hunger so strong that they could nearly kill a person with ambient feeding, but these are both extreme cases. The average vampire becomes dangerous to his donor only after repeated deeply intimate intercourse feeding sessions. This form of feeding, when done correctly, drains so much energy from the donor that it will take days for her to recover from a single session.

Any human should be warned before considering having intercourse with a vampire. On the outside vampires may seem like the fair-skinned and charming creatures of myth and fiction novels, but on the inside their spirits look like something born of worlds found only in Lovecraftian tales. Vampiric spirits are inhuman in a way that can never be fully put into words. This inhumanity can be experienced, though, and will be experienced by anyone who connects with a vampire on this intimacy level. When vampires participate in intercourse, they fully engage every part of their spirit, pushing their feeding tendrils deep into the core of their partners from every angle. It can be an extraordinarily violating experience for the donor, one that few are prepared for. A relationship of any kind with a vampire means dealing with her Hunger as well.

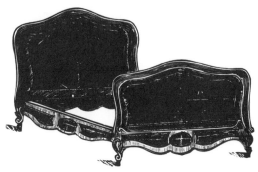

Bed Sharing

Even more intimate than the sexual act is the simple act of sharing a bed with a vampire. As the movie *Vampire Journals* and a few other films have suggested, when a vampire sleeps, his true face is revealed, metaphorically speaking. As the vampire sleeps, his conscious mind passes into a meditative dream state, releasing all control it has over the Hunger. The feeding tendrils, reacting in their normal and natural way, seek out any target within range and begin to feed. One would tend to think that a sleeping mind would be incapable of any kind of deep feeding, that it could not intentionally draw the energy out of a human. But the opposite is true: the sleeping mind of the vampire has an overall low frequency to match that of any other sleeping person, but it also has an extremely low amplitude in those frequencies that match humanity's. With the controls released, the vampire's spirit sucks in energy just as a black hole sucks in matter, consuming everything within its reach.

As with any other intimacy level, the only real danger to the donor with bed sharing is repeated exposure. One exposure will likely cause the human only to wake up a little more tired than usual, but sleeping in the same bed with a hungry vampire every night over a period of several months will cause a number of marked symptoms including a lack of REM sleep, a complete absence of refreshment from normal sleep, an inability to focus one's mind, and a persistent feeling of exhaustion. In essence, it is as close as a human will ever come to feeling what it is like to have the Hunger.

Clearly, there is only one way to lessen this intimacy level's impact on the human partner. The vampire must feed before bedtime from a source other than the partner. Of course, this will not fully prevent the feeding process, but it will make it more bearable.

It is important for the donor to remember that it is just as important for a vampire to release her grip on the Hunger while sleeping as it is to relax one's muscles during sleep, for the sake of the person's health and well-being. Just as going to bed tense will result only in stiff muscles or a crick in the neck, holding in the Hunger while a vampire sleeps could result in a dangerous energy blockage that could prevent effective feeding for days.

Deep Communion

Deep communion, the final and deepest intimacy level, is said to be a direct feeding from the core energies of the donor, and occurs when a vampire pushes his feeding tendrils all the way into one or more of a donor's chakras. This process is said to create a deep and permanent psychic link between the two partners. For days afterward the vampire should be able to hear his partner's thoughts at any given time, often when he does not even want to.

This is clearly not something that any vampire would enter into lightly. Most actually prefer to undergo this deep energy transfer when in a deeply committed relationship. They believe that truly being able to know someone inside and out with no walls or barriers between them is a unique and dangerous experience. For more information on deep communion, I refer readers to *The Psychic Vampire Codex*, by Michelle Belanger, where the term *deep communion* was first introduced.

Other Methods

There are other methods of psychic feeding that exist outside of the naturally progressive order of the intimacy levels. Primarily, these feeding methods exist outside of the order because, although they require a certain level of intimate knowledge or psychic connection with another person, they are not intimate acts in and of themselves. The first of these methods is dreamwalking. Michelle Belanger speaks extensively about dreamwalking in her book *Psychic Dreamwalking*. Dreamwalking occurs when a person uses a preexisting psychic bond to invade the sleeping mind of another, allowing herself to psychically communicate with the other person via the medium of dreams. If the initiator of the dreamwalk is alive, she must be asleep or in a deeply meditative state to dreamwalk successfully. Disembodied spirits naturally do not have this limitation, which is why the dead dreamwalk much more often than the living. For both the living and the dead, feeding through a dreamwalk proceeds in the usual way once the connection is made.

How does one tell a dreamwalk from a normal dream, especially when most dreamwalks occur unintentionally? Normal dreams have a natural haziness to them, not unlike a deep daydream—which comes from the fact that they originate in the creative and less detail-oriented parts of the brain. Even memories often come through much clearer, since they originally came from solid sensory perceptions that were permanently burned into the brain as if it were a CD. In effect, reality is simply more real than imagination.

Dreamwalks, on the other hand, go far beyond what the imagination can manifest. Even those rare few people who can feel intense pain in a dream or smell a lemon in a daydream are caught off guard by the sheer level of realism and detail comprehension in a true dreamwalk. Similar to dreamwalking is feeding through astral projection. A great many folktales, such as those regarding the Strigoi Morte, who travel as a spirit after they have died, or the Gillo of Lesbos, who shed their bodies as they sleep, claim that vampires often have fed in this manner, traveling without the need of a body to take energy directly. Remote feeding is a form of feeding that uses an existing bond with a human donor to feed, even when the donor is not in the immediate area. Proximity is still a factor in the feeding process, so this type of energy drain works well only when the bond is very strong.

This feeding method works much as any other. The vampire focuses the entirety of his mind on the target, connects with it through the preexisting bond just as he would a feeding tendril, and lowers his amplitudes to "suck" the energy in. If any strong emotion—love, hate, or anything similar—is the foundation of the bond, this feeding can go surprisingly well. It should be noted, however, that the target will likely lose significantly more energy than the vampire will gain, due to the many random disruptions that could come between the two individuals, so this method should be used only in an emergency.

Cycling, or *self-feeding*, describes any method by which a vampire recycles the energies already within her body or spirit. In technical terms, this is not actually a feeding process, since no new energy is taken in. Instead, it is more of a maintenance necessity for anyone who regularly deals with large amounts of energy that can easily become blocked, bogged down, or misrouted. Recycling interior energies helps to get the power to where it is most needed—those energy cores that support vital functions—which helps to subdue the Hunger.

CHAPTER 5

Blood Feeding

 History

Throughout the course of human history there have been a great many people from all over the globe who have voluntarily participated in the act of drinking blood. Most stick strictly to animal blood—that of goats and cows, usually—but some actually go so far as to drink the blood of their fellow humans. Elizabeth Bathory, for instance, supposedly drank blood from time to time, though she was primarily known for bathing in it. The Blood Countess, as she was known, killed dozens of peasant girls during her reign over a Hungarian county in the early seventeenth century in an attempt to use their blood and pain to maintain her youth and beauty. It is debatable whether she was a true vampire or simply a deranged human, but it was the Strigoi Vii rulers of the region that ended her bloody reign. Supposedly, it was King Matthias II who discovered her atrocities and sent a small army to take her down.

Blood drinking is not natural for humans. It is a practice that is always consciously entered into and most often done when there is no other choice. Certain African tribes, for instance, will bleed cows to avoid having to kill the animal. They greatly need the protein but cannot afford to slay the beast, because of both its monetary value and its ability to produce milk. There is a significant drawback to humans drinking blood. Human digestive systems cannot handle blood. Its iron content is too high. It is toxic to the human body, and so it operates as a natural emetic, coming back up as soon as the body realizes the danger.

Different groups combat this situation in different ways. Certain African tribes mix the blood with milk, honey, or even urine to help trick the body into accepting it while simultaneously coating the stomach to prevent too much of the iron from being absorbed. The Masai tribe of Kenya in particular is famous for drinking a mixture of cattle blood and milk during ceremonial warrior rites, such as coming of age ceremonies or before ritual battles. The blood is collected by firing an arrow at close range into the jugular vein of a cow, cutting it enough to fill a skin gourd with the vital substance. Later, the collected blood is mixed with milk and shared by the entire gathering. The tribe takes these rituals very seriously and rarely allow outsiders to witness them, though the rare few who have observed these rituals have taken copious video footage that can easily be found online. As for the ritually bled cattle, all cows involved in this ceremony are well taken care of, their wounds tended until fully healed. Cattle are much too valuable to the Masai for them to be allowed to bleed to death or die from infection.

People in other parts of the world even cook blood to make various interesting dishes, such as Black Pudding, a dish that is very common in modern Ireland, Scotland, and England. The recipe is simply blood cooked with some other filler until it is thick enough to congeal when cooled. In fact, blood sausages like Black Pudding have been around for as long as people have been slaughtering animals for food, and are even referenced in Homer's *The Odyssey*. Blood sausages naturally have many variations in many countries, like the "boudin noir" of France, a blood sausage made with brandy and cream. England and France each have a festival once a year dedicated to this dish, and the English festival includes a game that requires contestants to encase the sausages in women's tights and hurl them at a twenty-foot-high stack of Yorkshire puddings.

Tolerance

If the human body is unable to drink decent quantities of pure blood without mixing, diluting, or cooking it, and vampires are arguably physiologically human, then are vampires actually able to drink blood? In fact, vampires are quite capable of consuming considerable quantities of this usually toxic substance.

The question, then, is *why*? Why are vampires so capable of easily consuming and digesting a substance that the average human is not?

The answer may lie in the animal kingdom—specifically, the vampire bat. Vampire bats are capable of maintaining a diet of animal blood without succumbing to iron poisoning due to a thick mucus lining in their stomachs. The protein and other nutrients in blood are digested normally, but the excess iron is kept from entering the bat's system by the slimy substance and is quickly expelled from the body along with the majority of the blood's water, which otherwise would make the bat too heavy to fly.

Is it coincidence that many members of the modern vampire group the Strigoi Vii have reoccurring sinus problems throughout their lives? Sinus infections, excessive drainage, and a myriad of other nasal difficulties plague nearly every vampiric child until adulthood, and though this may not seem unusual for any child, the fact remains that all these symptoms are simply side effects of the vampires' unusually high level of mucus production.

Energy Transfer

So, what is it in the blood that contains this vitally untapped source of energy? The answer is simple: the iron itself. The very thing that makes blood toxic is what makes it desirable to vampires.

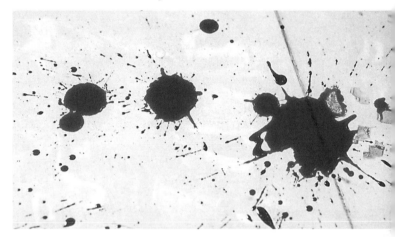

As blood circulates through the body, it becomes intimately connected with both body and spirit. It is what carries all of the body's nutrients, oxygen, water, and even hormones to their proper destinations, be-coming somewhat of a microcosm of the overall being as it does so. As it travels the bodily circuit, iron in the blood absorbs energy from the person's spirit, holding within it both the electrons and the vibrational pattern. Having been exposed to the entirety of the spirit, the electromagnetic pattern within blood is an amalgam of the frequencies of the entire spirit, rendering it a nearly unmodulated summary of that person. In a way, the energy in blood is pure.

As the vampire takes blood, the energy transfer commences in much the same way that it does in typical energy feeding. The vampire's spirit instinctively finds a sympathetic frequency and begins the drain. In many ways, though, blood feeding is more efficient than energy feeding.

When energy feeding, bonded frequencies are connected over a distance, which allows a certain amount of energy to be lost in the journey. The greater the distance, the more energy is lost. But with blood feeding, this is not the case. Since the blood itself is surrounded by the spirit, not one single stray electron is lost. Sympathetic frequencies surround it on all sides, transferring a significant amount of electromagnetic energy from even a small amount of blood. In essence, the donor loses less energy, yet the vampire receives the same amount.

When a donor is directly involved, there is also a certain amount of psychic feeding as well. Whether the blood is taken through a cut, a pierce, or even a bite, pain is involved, and pain can cause a rise in energy output. Even those who do not consciously energy-feed, or perhaps do not even have the training to do so, will naturally draw this excess energy in.

All in all, blood feeding has its advantages over energy feeding. It can be more efficient, requires less training, and is in essence a much simpler process. However, it is not without risks.

 Risks

First off, the drinking of human blood is illegal in most countries. In the United States, most states have laws specifically forbidding the drinking of animal blood, which is not nearly as fulfilling as human blood but can be useful in a bind, as well as laws against bleeding a human or drinking human blood.

Most viruses like HIV are extremely fragile and will not survive contact with the acid in human saliva, much less that of the digestive tract, and the human body has all manner of other systems to prevent infection by diseased food, including several forms of bacteria in the intestines specifically bred to fight harmful bacteria. Unexpected things happen, though. A cut in the mouth or an ulcer in the stomach opens the body up to dangerous attack. Whether a vampire is engaged in blood feeding or psychic feeding, he must always be selective about his donors. When blood feeding, this means always getting the donor tested for sexually transmitted diseases.

Viruses are not the only reason for being picky about donor choice when blood feeding. There is also the concept of bad energy. Sometimes people have energy that is modulated with frustration, panic, fear, hate, or any number of other generally negative emotions—so much so that these emotions suffuse their

flesh and blood. When psychically feeding, vampires can stop the process as soon as they realize that the energy is bad. With blood feeding, the energy transfer is completely internal, and is therefore nearly impossible to stop.

Beyond emotional, energetic, or viral problems, the blood is also capable of carrying various chemical substances that a smart vampire would likely not want to encounter. Drugs, both legal and illegal, and alcohol can be easily and effectively transferred from a human to a vampire through the consumption of blood, with virtually no reduction in their effects whatsoever. Hormones as well are likely to be transferred through sanguine feeding, though to a lesser effect. Hormone transfer would eventually cause the vampire to physically resemble the donor somewhat, particularly in facial features. The advantage here is that vampires do tend to pick beautiful donors.

The final risk when blood feeding is one that may not exist at all—the concept of "blood bonding." Some believe that blood feeding can lead to a psychic bond between vampire and donor, causing thoughts and emotions to be transferred between even near strangers. If this occurs, it is a result of the highly efficient energy-transfer process involved during blood feeding. The vampire could be intensely exposed to nearly every frequency within the human and might be able to use this to tap into the donor on a core level if she tried.

Downfall

In the end, blood feeding may have many appealing facets—its efficiency, its intensity, and especially its taste—but it is a fatally flawed process. Vampires are naturally designed to energy-feed, from the higher frequencies in their cores to the very tips of their tendrils. Blood feeding, however it began, was never, or perhaps should never have been, a substitution for direct energy feeding.

Blood feeding removes the necessity of sensing energy to feed and therefore prevents vampires from practicing as often as they otherwise would. Without the ability to tell good energy from bad, run-ins with unhealthy energy can only become more and more common.

The lack of practice with energy feeding can also cause one further problem. Vampires never lose the ability to psychically feed, using it to a certain extent even during blood feeding, though they can lose their ability to know when they are taking direct energy. When blood becomes scarce, this becomes dangerous. Survival becomes a priority, and the vampire's spirit, of its own unconscious accord, begins to take energy from every available source. Unaware that this drain is occurring, vampires are likely to do great damage to those closest to them before they realize what is happening.

The fact is that many vampires blood-feed, so much so that it has become a staple in the fictions about their kind for the last several hundred years. But the commonality of it should not be considered an endorsement, nor should it be considered an excuse to practice it. Vampires are by nature intelligent and ethical creatures, and as such they believe that those who choose to practice this method of feeding, whatever their reasons may be, do so in the most intelligent, discriminating, and clinically safe ways possible.

CHAPTER 6

Vampiric Abilities

Appearance

One of a vampire's greatest abilities is being able to seduce her prey, and much of that ability rests solely on simple appearance. Throughout the history of mankind, most of the mythologies about vampires describe them as tall and beautiful creatures with porcelain features and granite muscles. Anne Rice's Lestat is an excellent example of the modern version of this myth, but before him, there were the Sidhe, the Strigoi Vii, the incubi, the succubi, and many others. All of these were said to have soft hair, fair skin, full lips, and white teeth; most of all, they are always said to have intense, beautiful, piercing eyes. Stephenie Meyer's vampire saga *Twilight* may be the first story to make mention of skin that sparkles in sunlight.

Vampires, physically, are supposed to be quite gorgeous creatures, but are essentially physically the same as humans. Their spirit, however, varies distinctly. While a vampire's core structure is very similar to the average human's, with all chakras and basic structures in the same places and serving the same functions, his outer structure is very different.

For vampires, the layers of the spirit do not necessarily build up to a humanoid form that radiates an aura. The structure of their spirit may have developed as a method to store more energy, or to recycle and conserve power, or it may have other origins entirely. Regardless, most vampires find that the appearance of their spirit has more in common with an octopus than it does a human.

In essence, a vampire's spirit body is nothing more than a writhing mass of tendrils, slithering around one another and constantly molesting the surrounding environment. These tendrils play a major role in

The Weiser Field Guide to Vampires

the feeding process, and they are the only truly obvious sign of the existence of a vampire. Even those humans with barely any psychic sensitivity at all will often feel the tendrils when they come into contact with a vampire, though the human rarely has any idea what these "feelers" are that gently try to worm their way under the skin of anyone within their reach.

Others still are taken aback by the fact that on some level they can sense that vampires do not have auras. The vampire's Hunger does not allow many random electrons to escape the highly cohesive electromagnetic system we call the spirit, preventing any form of energy from radiating beyond the main structure. Whether it is called an aura or a halo, most people do not understand how much they are comforted by the existences of these fields until they encounter a person without one.

Physical Abilities

In modern times the vampire is well known for his physical strengths and abilities, although few of the older legends ascribe any of these qualities to the race, modern mythology—as presented in movies and novels—has greatly popularized this concept of the overpowering and physically unstoppable vampire: vampires like marble-muscled Lestat or the massive and monstrous version of Dracula that appeared in the third *Blade* movie. So it seems only fitting that we start there. Of course, it is important to remember that all

real vampiric abilities rely solely on the manipulation of electromagnetic energy to achieve their effects, but the abilities described in this section are of a more physical nature, the powers that result when a vampire's energy reserves are channeled into the physical realm.

Vampiric strength is one of the few commonalities of both modern and ancient mythologies of vampiric creatures, from the *Epic of Gilgamesh* to the television show *Tales from the Dark Side*, which featured a number of episodes dealing with vampires, including "Strange Love," which first aired in 1985. All of these fictions seem to have relatively the same concept, though: that vampires may be of basically normal human size and build but possess superhuman strength. Most of these fictions seem to hold to the idea that it is the spirit within the body that holds the strength, supercharging the muscles to go beyond their typical bounds. Bodybuilders and martial-arts masters train themselves to channel energy into their muscles and bones through mental focus and psychological connections to their bodies, pushing them to be stronger for a time.

As was evidenced by Lestat's flurry of violin playing in the movie *Queen of the Damned*, vampiric speed has also become a common theme in modern mythology. This was not always so, though. The closest thing to superhuman speed found in older myths is the concept of vampires moving nearly instantaneously from one place to another due to the lack of a body, one example being the *loogaroo* of Grenada, who shed their flesh at night and travel as a ball of fire.

Vampiric reflexes may also contribute to the idea of vampiric speed, and of the vampiric "flit"—a short burst of superhuman speed. The Strigoi Vii are quite well known for this. Their constant

interaction with the energies of the humans surrounding them, combined with their tendrils' tendencies to track movements and energy flows, gives them an advantage in emergency situations, allowing them to react almost before the situation begins to occur.

A good partner to vampiric reflexes is the concept of vampiric endurance. While the undead corpses of medieval folktales were not particularly known for their endurance, the massive power reserves of real vampires can be channeled into just about any activity. Whether running, lifting weights, or just having sex, modern vampires are known for being able to go longer and stronger than the average human, pushing their bodies past normal human limits for extended periods.

Vampirically fast healing abilities are another staple of modern mythology, allowing the starring characters to seem invincible, not being slowed down by cuts, blunt trauma, or bullets, even repairing fire damage with seeming ease. Unfortunately, real vampires are not gifted with this ability, at least not to this extreme level.

Some vampires are, however, very skilled at channeling their natural spiritual energies. And, like Reiki masters, they are capable of using these vast reserves to speed the natural healing processes of the body. It is possible through this kind of work to heal a cut, a bruise, or even a severe wound in a fraction of the time it would normally take. The vampiric ability to heal does have one extra factor that rarely gets displayed in movies or novels: their ability to heal others. Like a human healer, vampires can channel their energy reserves into those who are accepting and willing, and thereby heal them. However, the most effective means a vampire has for healing others is through the simple process of taking energy. Most disease is caused by blockages of energy and misaligned energy flows, so a vampire, by feeding gently on the diseased, can actually be quite helpful. A simple headache, for instance, can be cured by simply draining the built-up energy from the affected area. Once the blockage is gone, natural energy flow is restored.

To an extreme extent, this ability to heal through feeding can be used to purify a human's spirit and heal all ailments. As Bram Stoker's Dracula healed his victims of their weakness by ridding them of their humanity when he shared his blood with them, modern vampires can purify a human spirit through deep and intense feeding. For a time afterward, the human will be free of pain and will feel stronger than ever.

While popular fiction has not often addressed the vampire's ability to heal other people, it has certainly paid plenty of attention to a vampire's heightened senses. There is some truth to this myth. Some people are simply born with sensory gifts. For example, perfume companies seek out those who have an uncanny ability to distinguish between extremely subtle scents. Likewise, certain artists seem able to see the subtle differences in colors or patterns that few others can. And those who deeply care about music can train themselves to hear even the smallest change in tone or pitch.

Vampires may well have one sensory advantage over even well-practiced humans: their ability to see well in low light. Some vampires seem to be gifted with a high capacity for both night and color vision. Perhaps this complexity or advancement of the vampiric eye is responsible for their famously beautiful irises.

Vampires also can be spotted by their often above-average IQs. The ability to apply their high intellectual power to any situation, the gift of learning any skill quickly, and the general desire to consume all available knowledge are all common traits of the vampire.

Intelligence is primarily determined by two factors: memory and speed of thought. It is possible that the higher number of frequencies that vampires' spirits and minds operate on give them a higher capacity to retain memories, though this has little to do with the actual memories recorded in the brain. But the real memory advantage that vampires have is their uncanny ability to spontaneously recall past-life memories. What this means is that within a single lifetime, a vampire may have the knowledge and experience gained from dozens of other lifetimes, giving her an extraordinary number of memories to call upon to solve modern problems. Whether starting a small business, acting in a play, or even writing a book, a vampire can seem beyond her years in both the scope of her knowledge and the authority with which she commands it. This is likely where the relatively modern myth of vampiric immortality originates. The Sidhe and the Strigoi Vii are never talked about in the old legends as living forever, nor even is Bram Stoker's Dracula explicitly described as physically everlasting. It was the belief that these creatures could reincarnate, with all of their previous memories and powers intact, that gave rise to the immortality of Bela Lugosi's portrayal of the Count.

Some believe that past-life memories must surely

reside only in the spirit and not in the brain, making them unavailable for daily use and therefore useless when it comes to testing intelligence. But this is not correct: past-life memories do primarily reside in the spirit, but the stronger ones—

those that are emotional, violent, or exceptionally serene—reside in more powerful electromagnetic waves that are capable of impressing themselves into the electrically sensitive physical structure of the brain.

The other facet of intelligence—speed of thought—is helped by the fact that vampire spirits and minds use the usual human frequencies as well as higher frequencies. Studies of brain waves have shown that higher frequencies move faster in the brain and are more complex, which means they can carry more information at a time, all in all resulting in a mind that can internally transfer more information per second than the average human mind.

There is also one other factor that may contribute to vampiric intelligence: meditation. Regular meditation clears the mind, relaxes the body, and increases blood flow to the brain. Vampires deal with large amounts of energy on a daily basis, so regular meditation is a fairly common practice for them, since it gives them a chance to take a few moments to process that energy and clear their systems of blockages. Many vampires meditate on a monthly, weekly, or even daily basis; some do it only on days that they feed.

Shape-shifting is another common characteristic of the mythic vampire. Shape-shifting is the process of changing one's form or appearance in some way, such as making oneself into a bat or a wolf or even making oneself look like another person or hiding in plain sight like a chameleon. Although this is impossible to do in the real world, another form of shape-shifting is possible. Made famous by Bram Stoker's Dracula, this is the ability to grow younger. While modern vampires do not actually grow younger, they live by the belief that the flesh is heavily influenced by the spirit, particularly the flesh of those with powerful spirits, so if one feels timeless, one is more likely to look timeless. This timeless appearance is of course helped by the fact that most modern vampires maintain strict workout regimens to keep them healthy and fit.

Energy Abilities

More common in the older legends of vampires, such as those of the magical Sidhe and the nature-controlling Annunaki, are energy-based abilities, and it is no small coincidence that they are still the most common abilities that modern vampires possess. All vampires are naturally gifted with abilities that help them change, control, and even extinguish energies.

Every vampire is capable of storing within his spirit an extraordinary amount of electromagnetic energy. For this reason, vampires are often interested in and involved in magick work at a young age. Instinctively drawn to the metaphysical and ethereal, the young vampire can often be seen reading up on various magickal disciplines, beliefs, and spells, and he quickly finds that he has a talent for it.

For most vampires, the continual use of rituals and spells becomes unnecessary. Most vampires develop the ability to simply want something, will it to happen, and thereby make it happen. It is a combination of a focused mind and enough power to throw behind the desire that cause the manifestation or change. But it has to be true desire. And these massive power reserves can be dangerous. Some of the legends regarding vampires speak of them as creatures that create and spread disease; consider, for example, the theory that the Black Death was caused by reanimated vampiric corpses.

When a vampire feeds, her tendrils connect with another spirit and find a sympathetic frequency. To draw energy in, the vampire simply lowers the amplitude on her end of the electromagnetic wave and thereby pulls energy in. To stop feeding, or simply to help avoid feeding on those with unsavory energy, vampires flood energy into the sympathetic frequency until they can break the bond. But a problem can occur when the bond is not severable, usually because it has been formed by a deeply intimate relationship continuing over a long period of time. Flooding energy into a permanent bond does not break it the way it should. Instead, any energy a vampire pushes into the bond flows into the spirit at the other end. And if the vampire is powerful enough, this energy flow can overwhelm the bonded spirit, flooding its system with unusable, unprocessable energy. It corrupts the spirit and causes the physical body to fall severely ill in all manner of ways. Every weak point in the body becomes a target for dangerous buildups and blockages of energy.

Thankfully, for the most part a vampire's excess energy floods not into other people but into his environment, particularly his living environment. Some like to call this environment a *haunt*, but others refer

to it as a *lair* or a *haven*. Regardless of what people call it, though, it is simply the chosen surroundings of the vampire—where he eats, sleeps, lives, and sometimes resides even after his death. It is his safe place, where he can relax and let his shields down. When a vampire is well fed, the lowering of psychological and energetic boundaries—his shields—allows some of his energy to seep out into the environment. But this energy is not simply bare electrons. This energy still carries the vampire's personal frequencies, the pattern of his intellect, his very essence. As this seepage goes on over time, the wood of the house's framing and walls, even the concrete of the foundation, begins to mimic his patterns—so much so that when he again feels the Hunger and draws this residual energy back into himself, the house remains tuned to his patterns, vibrating with him.

For a vampire, having a haunt has many advantages. First, it can be used as an additional storage area for energy. Good feeding can sometimes be scarce, but a vampire can always rest assured that the pain of the Hunger will lessen within the walls of his own home. Second, the energy of the house is still the vampire's energy and is therefore under his control. A good haunt can provide protection and even help make psychic feeding a little more efficient when it occurs within its boundaries. Third, it helps to protect against the damages of the sun. Of course, most homes do well to keep out direct sun, but some find that even in a home with

many large windows, the high-amplitude energies of the haunt do very well to keep the damaging ultraviolet rays out but let much of the light in, not unlike the earth's own magnetosphere.

All this energy has a psychological effect as well. Most people are not used to being so thoroughly surrounded by a vampire's energy. It can be a disturbing experience for some, an exciting one for others. The telepathically gifted have a different reaction entirely, though. A vampire's ability to shield his energies works both ways, not only protecting others from his Hunger, but also preventing his own thoughts from being heard even by the most skilled mind readers. Over time, the haunt also takes on much of this shielding, which means that its energy field muffles the constantly intruding thoughts of those outside it. To the telepathic and empathic, this brief respite while within can provide quite an enjoyable relief.

Vampiric talents are not limited just to the projection of energy, though. They have all the same receptive psychic abilities as humans, and like humans, not all of them are particularly gifted psychically, and those that are do not always bother to develop these talents. Those that do, however, may find that the Hunger has an interesting effect.

Remote viewing, mind reading, and divination are all examples of receptive psychic abilities, or the psychic decryption of incoming electromagnetic signals. All of us, human and vampire alike, live in a world that constantly bombards us with electromagnetic waves, and many of these waves contain interesting or useful information. All we have to do is allow the energy in and then teach ourselves how to understand it. A human is very much like an antenna, or a satellite dish at best, capable of picking up only those signals that bump into it or are directed straight at it. Vampires, on the other hand, have a natural pull due to the Hunger. They constantly pull energy toward them, even energy that is unusable, bending it in their direction. And beyond that, their tendrils stretch out into the world around them and operate on more frequencies than humans, as if they had an array of antennas constantly picking up random signals on many wavelengths.

Telepathy for a vampire happens a bit differently than it does for a human. For humans, telepathy occurs when their brains—their antennas—bump into a decipherable signal. For vampires, telepathy often occurs as a part of the feeding process, which means that even the particularly psychically untalented still occasionally hear people say things that were not said at all, just thought loudly. And, as with most of vampires' spiritual interactions with humans, the key to their mind-reading ability is sympathetic frequencies.

Vampires feed via the bonds they create through sympathetic frequencies. But the electromagnetic waves of a spirit, just like radio waves, are primarily used to transmit information, which means that most, if not all, are highly modulated, leaving almost no clean waves in any individual's spirit. When vampires feed, however, they tend to relax and focus just on the feeding, which generally demodulates the bonded frequency. This means that the more modulated, higher-amplitude human waves that the vampire is connected to have a pretty solid chance of adjusting the vampire's waves, the random extra bits of the human's waves causing vibrations in the vampire's not unlike those a voice causes in an eardrum. The less psychically experienced Strigoi Vii will likely interpret these adjustments as sounds, and thereby experience them as such. It is always an interesting experience, and usually occurs only when they are not looking directly at the person.

Vampiric thought transfer can work in reverse as well, causing a kind of thought control. Vampires' power reserves give them the ability to raise their amplitudes higher than most humans can, which means that a modulated signal from a vampire on a bonded wavelength can override just about anything the spirit on the other end can send out. Usually this does not occur during intentional feeding, which is more often than not a peaceful process. Instead, it most often occurs during an argument or a debate—a situation in which a vampire's aggressive, predatory nature begins to peek out and push energy toward his or her opponent. This is not a subtle process. It is not an influencing of another's mind. It is an aggressive domination of the energies and the very intellect of another spirit.

At the very least, the opponent will respond aggressively—an instinctive reply to a slight feeling of intimidation. At the worst, the opponent will cease to fight back. Feelings of confusion and fear pervading their minds, they will likely have some awareness that their thoughts are being entirely overpowered and will choose to back off instead of risking permanent damage. Repeated thought control of one person is never advisable. It can lead to a near-permanent sense of confusion in the victim, and an inability to retain his own thoughts or make decisions. Vampires generally believe that thought control in this manner is highly unethical and not worthy of a vampire's time or energy, regardless of how easy it is for them to achieve.

A better form of mental control is the simple power of adoration, a vampire's ability to get people to pay attention to her, enjoy her company, and even love her. Similar to the power that causes a vampire to seem familiar, this ability comes in handy for any number of situations—everything from getting a date to getting a job. But instead of the inward draw of the Hunger, which causes the familiar feeling toward vampires that some humans get—adoration is caused by broadcasting higher-amplitude, low-frequency waves, a broadcast combination usually resulting from the intense peacefulness of true confidence. The low-frequency flood of power induces an artificial meditative state in receptive individuals, pushing them into a somewhat relaxed and hypnotic mind-set, and making them generally open to suggestion and feeling quite good. On top of that, the gentle flow of energy and the use of lower, more common frequencies allow the human target to absorb much of the energy, taking it in and using it instead of being overwhelmed, bogged down, or sickened by it. Unused to this excess energy, the human may begin to feel light-headed or energized, as if experiencing a gentle but strong adrenaline rush. It is easy to become addicted to this experience. It is also easy for some to confuse this addiction with love.

 ## The Beacon

Modern vampires claim to have a natural ability to sense one another when in close proximity. They call this the *beacon* and theorize that it results from the natural flow of energy between two spirits of the same kind.

Not only is the beacon sensed as an energy flow; it has a psychological effect as well. In fact, when a vampire senses the beacon, the effect is similar to what humans feel when they are under the spell of a vampire's adoration ability. The vampire's attention is naturally, and sometimes subconsciously, drawn toward the other vampire as the energy flow creates a sense of attraction and fixation. Energy passes between the two vampires so easily that there is an instant sense of familiarity, in some cases even a familial closeness; and in truth. the two are family. In fact, all vampires are family. They share a bond that humanity will never have and that no human will ever experience apart from what he feels for his closest relatives and loved ones.

However, this bond works only in close proximity —usually never at a distance of more than one hundred feet or so, depending on how many obstructions are in the way. The higher a frequency is, the more likely it is to be disrupted by environmental influences, and vampiric frequencies are high enough that they may be relatively easily hindered by walls or environments with too much sunlight unless they are intentionally amplified to break through. Of course, it is also possible for a vampire to

train herself to be more sensitive to the beacon, learning how energy transfer feels on different wavelengths and amplitudes to a point that she will notice even a little energy conveyed through a vampiric frequency.

It is good that vampires have this familial bond. It gives them a sense of community even when they see each other rarely, and this sense of community is often the only comfort they have in a world that so often rejects them without trying to understand them. Human spirits are made up of electromagnetic energy, and like all energy, the energy of these spirits cannot be destroyed, only changed. The spirit itself can be destroyed, however—drained or disrupted to a point where its energies lose cohesion and disperse. Vampires are made of the same energy, but the Hunger—the ability and need to feed—gives them the opportunity to evolve faster, changing and adapting to new situations. It gives them the potential to contain more energy on more frequencies, allowing them a greater resistance to disruption and dispersal. It gives them a chance to feed from other spirits to repair damage that has been done or to replenish the energy reserves that have kept their spirits alive for thousands of years. As they have continued to exist, vampires have witnessed millions of human spirits fail and fade away. Their ability to feed has, in essence, given immortality to those strong enough, wise enough, and adaptable enough to take it.

CHAPTER 7

Vampiric Weaknesses

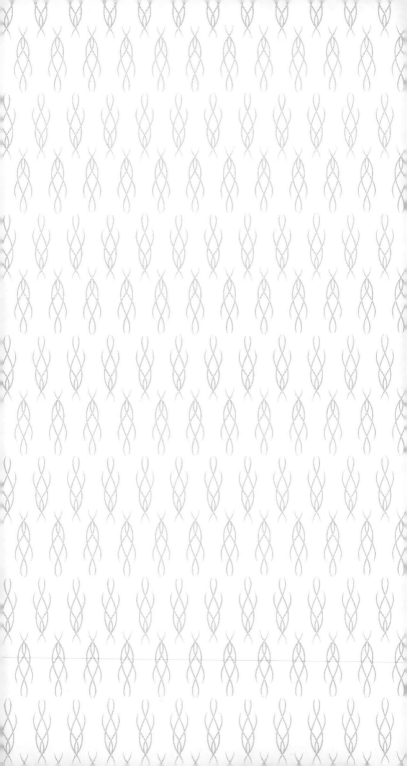

Vampires believe that not all darkness can be repelled by light. They say there is light and dark within every person and that each person must find her own balance between the two, a twilight path. However, to do this, vampires must understand not only their abilities, but their weaknesses as well.

Some members of the vampiric community may have concerns about the inclusion of a chapter describing their weaknesses, but this worry is unnecessary. Self-proclaimed hunters are not a major concern for the community. Most are harmless, rarely hurting anyone and often quickly turning tail and running once they encounter a true vampire, never to try again.

 Myth vs. Reality

There are quite a large number of alleged weaknesses surrounding the vampiric race. Some are real. Some are not. So, it seems a good idea to start by dispelling a few of the more common myths.

Take, for instance, the stake through the heart. Real vampires are not in any way undead or the walking dead. They are Strigoi Vii, living vampires. Any significant amount of damage is likely to kill them. Car accidents, bullet wounds, airplane crashes, and blunt trauma to the head are all things that will kill a vampire just about as easily as a human. Vampires are certainly more likely to be able to avoid these situations or to react quickly enough to save themselves if possible, but if the worst happens, major damage will do the job just fine.

So where does this legend come from? If a person was trying to keep a corpse from reanimating, stopping the heart from beating again, or simply pinning the corpse to the earth, would certainly do the trick. And for the scam artist "vampire hunters" of the Middle Ages, sharp sticks were easier to get hold of than silver crucifixes or blessed items.

Speaking of blessed items, they are another myth. Crosses, holy water, and items of faith or purity or belief do absolutely nothing to real vampires. Not even a human's faith in these items or in his deity will provide him with a weapon against vampires. Human energy is human energy. Vampires can feed on faith as easily as they can on love, lust, or anger.

Another interesting myth is the one surrounding mirrors. Clearly, since vampires are physical creatures, a vampire's image will appear in reflective surfaces as easily as will that of any other creature, and the European tradition of covering mirrors after the death of a loved one shows a common belief that disembodied spirits can be seen in reflective surfaces easier than with one's own eyes. If real shape-shifting werewolves had existed during the late Middle Ages, as so many legends claim, it would have been in their best interest to start the rumor that it would take a silver bullet to kill them. After all, the countryside farmers were the only people who would have reason to go werewolf hunting, and they were the people least likely to be able to afford the silver and the gun, and the least likely to have the skill to make the silver into bullets. Those who could afford the tools to hunt those vicious beasts—the nobility and city-dwelling craftsmen—would have had no reason or desire to waste large sums of money and risk their lives chasing a dangerous animal.

The same logic applies to real vampires and the expensive silver-backed glass mirrors of the time period. Even if they believed the myth, the poor would not have bothered to chase after vampires, since they had no way to specifically identify a vampire. And the wealthy would have had little or no desire to do so. Of course, it is also true that vampires throughout history have often made their livings as artists, actors, writers, dancers, and craftsmen of all kinds, not to mention that real vampires have often been born to the noble bloodlines of

Europe. So should one of these Strigoi Vii have feared that her vampiric nature was discovered, all she would have had to do was publicly gaze into her own mirror.

A final myth is the idea of the counting vampire. Today, this concept is not very well known, because, outside of a certain purple-skinned puppet that lives on *Sesame Street*, modern mythology does not give it much attention. A vampire story of the early or mid-Middle Ages would not have been complete without it, though. The people of the time seem to have believed that all vampires were obsessive-compulsives. They were not exactly wrong.

The Middle Age legends of Europe openly proclaimed that a vampire could be barred from entering through a doorway by spreading salt, sand, millet, or seeds in front of it, because the vampire would not be able to pass through until he had counted every last granule, or at least cleaned up the mess. Another legend professed that a sure sign of a vampire having been in your house was that every shoelace and knot in the home had been untied. These legends may seem absurd today, but consider the fact that someone with high intelligence will often exhibit obsessive-compulsive behavior if his mind is not continually stimulated. And while modern vampires do not believe that their kind have ever been prone to invading homes, it is hard to think of a situation less mentally stimulating than that in which most people of the Middle Ages found themselves— one in which education and literacy were so rare that they were often considered a waste of time for anyone other than those joining religious institutions.

Sunlight

While modern vampires are certainly in no danger of spontaneous combustion, all vampires mythical and real are sensitive to sunlight to one degree or another, even if the only danger is in revealing their vampiric nature as their skin begins to sparkle like diamonds, as is true of the vampires in the *Twilight* saga. For real vampires, it starts with simple light sensitivity. For the most part, vampiric eyes are adapted more to low-light environments, making vampires much more comfortable in twilight times of the day rather than at noon. The effects of sunlight can often cause pain and exhaustion in the eyes, but this is nothing compared to the nausea that follows. Some even have strong skin reactions such as severe sunburns or even blisterlike bumps. Extended exposure to sunlight can also lead to a feeling of great weakness, pain, headaches, and even vomiting.

Some of these symptoms can be explained away as a simple lack of conditioning to solar radiation, easily remedied with a good pair of sunglasses and regular visits to the tanning bed. But the majority of these ailments stem from how intense ultraviolet radiation affects the spirit. All spirits are sensitive to the high-frequency, chaotic force of the sun. This is why most of the disembodied prefer the indoors and are always more active after the sun has begun to set.

Living humans have two advantages when it comes to sun sensitivity. The first is that their spirits operate on lower frequencies than vampires'. Lower frequencies are less easily disrupted, so it is the higher frequencies, those that make a vampire a vampire, that are more at risk for disruption and that can cause vampires to leak energy. The other advantage is that a human spirit is contained completely within its body, emanating only loose energy as an aura, throw-off energy, and spiritual exhaust, so no important parts of the spirit itself are ever exposed to direct sunlight. Vampire spirits are larger than human spirits, so the main body often expands a little farther than the flesh, despite the fact that they appear smaller due to the lack of an unnecessarily large aura; and the tendrils are always fully exposed, constantly wafting around in the air around them.

There are a number of ways a vampire can protect herself from solar damage, ranging from the physical—sunglasses and sunscreen—to the spiritual—energy shielding and intentionally withdrawing the spirit deep into the body. Damage is still sometimes done, though. Short-term exposure to intense ultraviolet radiation can cause disruptions in the outer layers of the spirit that may take time and meditation to heal. Long-term or excessively repeated exposure can cause much bigger problems. If deeper layers of the spirit are damaged, internal energy leakage can occur. Similar to internal hemorrhaging, such leakage can cause large amounts of energy to flow into places it should not, creating blockages, buildups, and counterproductive energy flow. Sometimes, these internal leaks worm their way to the surface through weakened areas of the upper layers, causing the energy to spew out into the environment.

In cases like these, active steps must be taken to correct the leak and avoid the unnecessary physical weakness and health problems that would otherwise occur.

 Iron

It appears that the ancient Celtic tribes were the only people to have discovered the vampiric weakness against the element iron. Many of the legends about vampires and iron are absurd tales about leaving a piece of lodestone—magnetic iron ore—in the doorway when entering the home of a Sidhe so he cannot close and seal the door behind the unsuspecting human. The truth is, a blade of iron can indeed do more than physical damage to a vampire, and magnetically charged bits of iron worn as jewelry can interfere with the feeding process.

Just like everyone else, vampires require iron in their diets. In fact, as mentioned before, their adaptations actually allow vampires to safely consume more iron than the average human, and a good portion of the vampire population prefer to get their energy from the iron in human blood. Their dislike of iron does not stem from an allergic reaction. It comes from the metal's ability to easily gain and maintain a strong magnetic charge, which is in fact also why many magickal practitioners avoid the metal when choosing their ritual items. Inside the human body, the small bits of the element easily take on the holder's personal electromagnetic frequencies, but outside the body it tends to be resistant to taking on a personalized frequency, instead maintaining only a basic magnetic charge, which can be disruptive to any flowing electromagnetic wave.

Just as the earth's magnetosphere fends off the electromagnetic radiation of the sun, so, too, can a metal imbued with the earth's magnetism fend off the electromagnetic waves of a vampiric spirit. A lodestone amulet worn around the neck could operate as a small force field, repelling or disrupting a feeding tendril that comes near it. Similarly, an iron blade, polarized to have an electrostatic charge, could leave a wound in a vampire's flesh that he would likely have a lot of trouble healing. The magnetic field not only would hinder the vampirically inclined from directing energy to the area to heal the wound itself, but would also likely interfere with the natural flow of the vampire's spirit, which could prevent him from using his energies to augment his strength, speed, and endurance. Of course, the wound itself would have to be pretty severe, perhaps life-threatening, to be effective against a vampiric spirit, but if an individual had intentions of attacking a Strigoi Vii, this would be the way to go. This may be why some Celtic legends state that only a weapon of iron could kill a Sidhe. This is certainly not the only thing that can kill a vampire, but it will do a better job than most.

Oddly enough, this vampiric weakness also happens to be the source of a number of other myths, the most obvious of which is that of the lucky horseshoe.

An old Irish myth states that a horseshoe hung above a doorway is supposed to prevent any Sidhe from crossing the threshold and repel unwelcome magick. It is ironic, though, that even most vampires are unaware of this weakness, since it is the one with the most potential for harm and hindrance. This could be attributed to the fact that most people in the modern era simply have no contact with iron ore. It can be used as a powerful defense against a vampiric attack, but it's just not easily found these days. On a day to day basis, the average vampire will always be more concerned about sunlight, starvation, or even their own psychic sensitivities.

Psychic Sensitivity

To survive, all vampires must interact with the energies of other creatures, particularly humans, so it should be no surprise that all modern vampires are naturally psychically inclined individuals. Their feeding process is designed to take the energies of others into themselves and incorporate them into their beings, so it is perfectly understandable that they may be prone to picking up the occasional stray thought here and there. This ability is amplified further by the concept that human psychics only have one antenna, the brain, to use to pick up other human signals, whereas a vampire's tendrils operate as an antenna array, picking up dozens of thoughts on dozens of frequencies at any one time. Human psychics can rarely tune into more than one frequency at any particular moment, though they do often describe a constant background noise caused by other thoughts washing around in their immediate area.

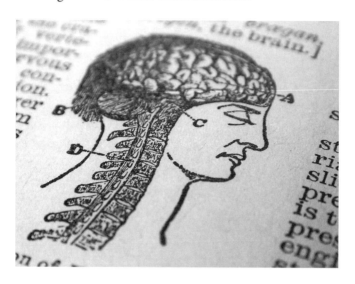

In a lot of ways, this psychic sensitivity may seem like a gift, and it can be, but only after years of practice to control it. In fact, an inexperienced young vampire may often find himself emotionally reacting to others' thoughts, sharing other people's emotions, or responding to unspoken thoughts. To many, this psychic ability is nothing more than an oddity or a novelty. The young vampire simply has to learn how to keep his mouth shut until he can either learn how to differentiate thoughts from actual spoken words or simply block out human thoughts altogether. A few will always get through, though. Even after years of experience, the average modern vampire claims to still have occasional incidents in which particularly loud thoughts from people standing within range of his tendrils come through as full auditory hallucinations.

The vampire population seems to have a high percentage of empaths—those who are psychically sensitive to the emotions of others. For empathic vampires, it can become particularly difficult to deal the random emotions picked up from every person walking by. In fact, until they gain a little practice with their abilities, they will have a hard time even telling the emotions of others from their own. The outside feelings seep in through the subconscious mind of the vampire, pulling her mind in random directions. On a daily basis, this can begin to feel like a dissociative disorder—anything from bipolar disorder to schizophrenia—which can be difficult to deal with on its own, but it can get so much worse. In crowded public places, an empath can get overwhelmed by confusion, disorientation, and especially panic attacks.

Most vampires learn how to deal with their psychic impressions on their own. Some actively seek balance with their gifts through meditation; some feel their way through these new impressions until they can use this gift, understanding the thoughts and emotions coming from others and even using them to help the feeding process; and some simply learn to use their own more powerful spirit to overpower and block out the thoughts of others, shutting down these psychic sensitivities until they eventually get so close to someone that they have no choice but to pick up on the various thoughts and feelings of their loved one.

 Human Food

Clearly, human food does not have enough energy to fuel a vampire spirit, and when a vampire gets particularly starved for energy, other problems occur. The body begins to reject food, usually passing it through the system nearly undigested, and sometimes even immediately vomiting it back up as if it were poisoned. It seems that in this situation vampires react in the same way a person in a prolonged state of starvation does. They still want the food, knowing that the fuel within it would help somewhat, but they find themselves too weak to process it. The only solution for a vampire is for her to feed enough to sate the Hunger. Once she has accomplished that, her normal digestive capabilities tend to return.

Of course, even when a vampire's energy needs are taken care of, his system can still be quite picky. Some vampires tend to stick to a more vegetarian diet of low-energy vegetables, fruits, and grains. These items are easy to digest, keep the system clean, and provide most of the vitamins and nutrients the body needs. The low-grade energy of plant life teaches the vampire to gather the majority of his energy through feeding on other spirits, using the body's digestive process as a means to gather only the minerals the body needs.

Energy Quality

For the most part, the vampiric feeding process destroys any diseases within the energy taken in. Disease itself usually consists only of blockages of energy, but sometimes certain diseases more or less have a life of their own. They exist within the body, constantly trying to exert their influence not only in the body but also in the spirit, where the frequencies of the spirit begin to take on the disease's pattern. Mental diseases, even temporary ones like depression, are particularly bad about influencing the spirit, but even diseases that affect the spirit rarely have any effect on the feeding process. By their very nature, diseases, viruses, and mental problems cause a lowering of amplitudes in the spirit, not a heightening, so the modulation is not strong enough for a disease to be transferred to the vampire.

Prolonged disease or disorder may become transferable, though. People sometimes get stuck in bad places in their lives. Depression sinks in or jealousy becomes a way of life, and the spirit gets corrupted, modulated with these negative patterns and projected at high amplitudes. This is when a disorder becomes transferable, overriding and repatterning the low-amplitude sympathetic frequency of the vampire. This poisoned energy is transferred to the vampire in the same way thoughts can be, causing her to immediately become ill, which is precisely why most vampires are incredibly selective when choosing their donors, preferring to go hungry rather than risk unwarranted sickness.

 Relationships

Romantic relationships are often one of a vampire's greatest burdens. Vampires are powerful and unique creatures, so for them, true partnerships do not come easily.

The difficulties vampires have in relationships with humans should be obvious. Often, humans become overly drained even if their vampiric partner is careful about staying well fed from outside sources. For a vampire, spending any significant amount of time with a human and allowing herself to become emotionally bonded with a partner will eventually expose that person to the vampire's Hunger, no matter how careful both partners are. The human will become weak and sick as he begins to feel a form of the Hunger himself, and in some cases he even becomes obsessed with the vampire, creating an unhealthy, jealous, and codependent relationship.

The other prime difficulty with human relationships is fear. Vampires do well to keep their predatory natures well below the surface, hidden behind the mask of humanity they wear. But long-term relationships require spending a lot of time with the other person, and spending that kind of time with someone means that at some point the partner will see the vampire at his best and worst. As the character Edward of *Twilight* fame discovered, it is impossible for a vampire to resist feeding on those closest to him for long.

Many vampires believe that a romantic relationship with another vampire will always be more rewarding, though often more difficult to find. For those who grew up in, or frequently travel to, large cities like Atlanta, New York, or San Francisco, finding others of one's own kind is relatively easy, but the other sixty or seventy percent often find that running across another true vampire is a rare occasion. There are seldom more than one or two of them in any smaller city, though there are often many who claim to be, and despite the familial bond they all seem to have, there is no guar-

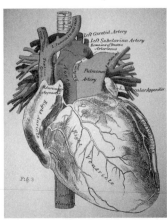

antee that two who may find each other will get along.

In the end, any person can certainly survive without a lifetime-long relationship. A person does not necessarily need a partner to be happy and successful, but the constant struggle to find one is what causes the weakness in vampires. Their physical health is strongly dependent upon their mental state, and the constant distress and depression of failure of this sort, of having one's heart repeatedly broken, can cause life-threatening sickness. For a vampire, being heartsick is a very real and dangerous condition.

Oddities

Anyone who has ever done regular work with powerful energies knows about all the odd little things that happen when that energy gets loose. Batteries can randomly charge themselves or go dead, computers can crash or even catch fire, and occasionally objects go flying across a room. The excessive amounts of energy in vampires' spirits cause these things to happen every day.

For vampires, computers are the worst of it. Computers are completely made up of tiny, easily disrupted, electrically sensitive components. The high power levels of a vampire's spirit interact with these components, usually in negative ways, and cause random and unpredictable results. Most often, the computer simply slows down or does not do what it is supposed to do, particularly when the vampire is stressed. Sometimes it is worse, though. One vampire in particular claimed that she used to stay so constantly stressed that she could not touch a computer without crashing it and somehow wiping the hard drive clean. Others have been known to do the same with cell phones on occasion.

Mostly, these disruptions and oddities are caused by electromagnetic pulses created by the vampire's brain. When a person gets mentally stressed in one way or another, whether that be the negative stress of frustration and anxiety or the more positive stress of trying to solve a problem or work out how to express something in writing, energy begins to build up inside the person's head. For the average human, this buildup of energy will do no more than cause a headache, but for the average vampire the buildup is often strong enough to escape the confines of the brain, and it does so in bursts, or pulses. What this means is that the normally smooth and harmless energy waves a vampire's spirit usually radiates turn into battery-draining, computer-crashing, fluorescent-lightbulb-frying electromagnetic pulses, and the stronger the spirit, the stronger the pulses can be. On one occasion, a vampire was witnessed discharging every battery within a ten-foot radius and significantly draining the charge of many that were twenty feet away. On another occasion, one of their kind was seen severely interfering with the operation of several fluorescent lights, the most distant of which was about forty feet away. By the next day, half the bulbs had blown, and none ever regained normal operation. Needless to say, many vampires find that they cannot wear wristwatches on a regular basis.

Vampires cannot live as hermits and hill people, avoiding modern society and all its trappings. Their Hunger will not allow it. So, they adapt and they deal.

Every living creature will experience emotional outbursts and stress at one point or another; it is inevitable. But vampires can take steps to reduce these occurrences. Regular meditation is always helpful, and for those who have particular trouble with computers, at least ten  minutes of mind-clearing meditation before the computer is even switched on is often recommended. Emotional detachment is also helpful. Maintaining an emotional distance between oneself and one's daily routine can help to prevent stress buildup, and as always, a warm bath, a good massage, or even doing a good deed can help prevent random electromagnetic pulse surges. It is all about self-control and intelligent stress relief.

Facade

Several times now the human mask that vampires wear has been mentioned, the facade of humanity that they use to blend in with society. But never before has it been referred to as a weakness. Not only does it take time, energy, and focus to maintain an effective illusion, not to mention a modicum of acting ability, but it also takes skill and experience, both of which are often gained through the repeated trial and error.

Mastery in the use of the facade can be achieved, but perfection will never be attained. There will always be flaws in the system, cracks through which a vampiric nature can be seen. Any show of anger, passion, or any other strong emotion will risk revealing a vampire's nature to the world. Beyond that, most humans also have a minor amount of psychic ability, and though most will never try to harness this gift, they are still affected by it subconsciously. In ways they do not comprehend, most humans will feel the predator behind the mask and fear it, and on some deeper level they may even feel it when they are being fed on, or know they are being watched by a hungry monster.

The facade is far from perfect, but it remains useful. Even those of the vampire race who are open to the world about their vampiric natures still do their best to maintain human behavior patterns at all times as a simple consideration for the feelings and comfort of the humans they encounter. For the most part, the vampire community wants the greater whole of humanity to openly accept them for who and what they are, but the process of acceptance takes time, and many in the community believe that it may never be achieved if they blatantly flaunt their worst predatory instincts.

CHAPTER 8

False Vampires

The first seven chapters of this book have been devoted to detailing precisely what a vampire is and is not, and the many myths that surround vampires. Their needs, abilities, and weaknesses, a bit of their history, quite a lot about their daily lives, and even a little about their physical appearance have all been described here. Still, though, there is a great deal of confusion out there regarding who is and who is not a real vampire.

Some of this confusion obviously stems from those who claim to be vampiric but are not. There are also those whom the general public mistakes for vampires but who have never claimed the title themselves. And, as always, there are a number of perfectly natural phenomena that the ignorant and uneducated claim to be vampiric attacks. This chapter is intended to sort through all the nonsense and expose false vampires for what they really are, friend or foe.

Claimers

Whether they do things to have energy directed at them or take it directly through physical contact and energy manipulation, energy addicts feel a rush, a high, from the energy they take in. Like adrenaline junkies, these people manipulate natural processes to achieve an addictive fix, and the energy they acquire is extremely addictive.

The human spirit is not designed to carry this level of energy, though, so the extra energy grounds out and dissipates into the environment, usually taking some of the human spirit's own energy with it and even doing damage to the spirit in the process. This causes the human to "crash," leaving him at a lower level than where he started, naturally filling him with the desire to immediately take more.

Energy addicts are fairly easy to identify. They get excitable after taking energy, like a child on a caffeine high. They will often describe the process as giving them a "charge," whereas real vampires usually get sleepy after feeding as their spirits turn their focus to processing and digesting the new energies, just as the physical body reacts after a heavy meal. It is also common to find energy addicts in positions of religious, social, or psychological authority. Though most preachers and psychologists do not claim to be vampires, many of them gain an energetic and psychological high when they incite emotional responses from a crowd.

Another common self-styled vampire is the blood fetishist, a person who regularly uses blood in sexual acts and perhaps cannot even become aroused without it. Whether it is the smell, the texture, or the look of blood that turns them on, fetishists all behave in the same way when in its presence. They become excitable and impatient. They enter into a kind of frenzy, their minds going a dozen different directions at once, over-whelmed by all the possibilities—precisely the opposite behavior one finds in a true vampire. A true blood-drinking vampire, like any predator, becomes both physically and mentally quiet, tightly focused, when in the presence of prey. The feeding process is not about excitement for them, and not about sex. It is about finding the most efficient way to get what they need. Even those modern vampires who use intercourse as a method to psychically feed do not precisely equate the act with pleasure, and those vampires who blood-feed are always clean and clinical with the process. For them it can be fun, a good bonding experience, but never sexual. It should also be noted that while some fetish-ists enjoy the taste of blood, they are still human and do not possess the adaptations of the vampire. Fetishists are therefore easy to identify due to their inability to consume more than a token amount of blood. To a real vampire, fetishists are often considered simply wasteful.

Another *false* vampire is the person who has fallen victim to sympathetic vampirism. When a vampire has fed from a person too much or too often, the prey will begin to experience symptoms similar to the Awakening. He will share the vampire's sun sensitivity, some of her predatory nature, and especially her Hunger. The energy taken from the human needs to be replaced, so the human begins to learn how to take energy from others just as the energy addicts do—though usually without overdoing it and grounding out, and thus turning it into a full-fledged addiction. Once the energy is replaced, the condition will clear up on its own, as will the belief that he is a true vampire. The human will return to his normal life, believing the entire incident to have been a simple misinterpretation of events.

The human's return to normality, however, is entirely dependent upon the vampire's ceasing to feed upon the prey, which is not as easy as it sounds. If the prey were just a friend or a donor, the feeding would have stopped long before it reached this dangerous level. Most sympathetic vampires are emotionally close to the vampire, deeply connected with her, and bonded to her in a permanent way. Energy will flow between vampire and human whether they like it or not, so either the vampire can push energy into the human, curing the sympathetic vampirism while simultaneously making the human sick with her energy, or the vampire can take energy from the human. If the vampire continues to take energy, she simply has to be mindful not to take too much. There is a right amount, just enough to encourage the other person's natural ambition and drive, but not enough to cause him to feel the Hunger. Of course, the best solution is a balanced give-and-take between vampire and human, but unfortunately, experienced psychic vampires have found that humans do not seem to be able to process and incorporate into their own spirits the higher frequencies of the vampire. Instead, the vampiric energies effectively taint and overpower the human's own energies. It can be thought of in terms of slowly dropping food coloring into a fishbowl: eventually, the human's water is all deeply colored.

Similar to sympathetic vampires are the *turned*. While sympathetic vampires are under the general impression that they were always vampires and have just now Awakened, the turned fully believe that they were once human and have now been turned into vampires. Although this is really just another form of sympathetic vampirism, these people are a breed apart.

Normal sympathetic vampires are generally logical, intelligent, and sane. They may be mistaken about their nature, but the vampire community at large still considers them to be good people, loved for their contributions to the community and their acceptance of the vampiric race. Like true vampires, they are skeptical by nature and accept the truth when it is revealed. The turned, however, fully embrace the concept that a spirit's basic nature and needs can be changed at the core level. They think that the Hunger gives them power, and in truth it does to a certain degree. But they abuse it: they feed irresponsibly and indiscriminately. And should they ever be confronted with the truth—that they are simply energy-addicted humans—they will refuse to believe it. Instead, they will continue to feed from others, increasing their developing energy addiction, all the while clinging to their "master," a true vampire who chose the wrong person to feed on.

The Mistaken

Besides those humans who claim to be vampiric, there are also a number of people who are sometimes mistaken by the public for vampires, or rather, by those people in the human population who are knowledgeable about modern vampires. Most of these people do not claim to be vampiric at all, and many have never even heard of real vampires. The falsely Awakened are a prime example of this phenomenon.

The falsely Awakened are individuals who do not possess a vampiric spirit or its Hunger but nonetheless begin to experience certain physical symptoms of the Hunger. Though these people have not been fed upon, they are often, not coincidentally, related to vampires or descended from known vampiric bloodlines.

Vampirism is a primarily spirit-based condition, but this book has also covered some of the physical and specifically genetic components that go along with it as well. Vampire spirits, like all spirits, create minor genetic changes in the bodies they inhabit. These traits are passed on to their children, but often they are useful only to a vampire. In fact, some can be controlled only by a vampire. So for the most part, these traits remain dormant in the human descendants, becoming evident only when another vampire is born into the bloodline. This is but one of the reasons that vampires and most human spirits stick to certain bloodlines: they can collect on their investments and stick to bodies that are more compatible. Unfortunately, there are occasions when certain vampiric genetic traits become active in a nonvampiric spirit. The human can experience agonizing pain, physical weakness, mental disorientation, and a number of other symptoms. Thanks to the research of the Atlanta Vampire Alliance, we now know that fibromyalgia, a nerve disorder that causes severe pain and has no known cause or cure, occurs in disproportionately high numbers among vampires, so it should be no surprise that it is a common ailment of the falsely Awakened.

What is it then that can cause a false Awakening? Although the answer is not entirely clear, one possibility is overexposure to situations that might entice vampiric genetics to become active, situations like predatory behavior or a nighttime-oriented lifestyle. Hematologists seem to be at particular risk of a false Awakening. Their exposure to so much blood and the energy within on a daily basis could cause even the smallest amount of vampiric genetics to respond in some way.

Drug addicts—or any addicts, for that matter—have symptoms similar to the Hunger. When their addiction is not fed, they experience pain as well as mental fatigue and, depending on the drug, a sense of exhaustion. Of course, these symptoms are only superficially similar to what modern vampires experience, but it is easy to see why someone might draw parallels and mistake typical substance abuse with the Hunger, or why a young vampire might mistake his own Hunger for an addiction. Experienced vampires believe that their need is not and has never been an addiction. The need does not go away after a "detox" period, though it may seem so to an onlooker as she watches a vampire adjust to going without. Instead, vampires' symptoms come back later even stronger. Nor should anyone confuse a vampire's sometimes pale and gaunt appearance with the similar appearance of a drug user. The vampire community does not condone the use of illicit drugs or the abuse of legal ones. Vampires' appearance, though sometimes striking, is natural and not at all chemically induced.

Finally, the greatest number of people mistaken by onlookers for being vampiric are those who are most accepted by the vampires themselves, the friends of the vampiric community. A friend of the community, sometimes called a *swan*, is any person who is aware of the existence of vampires and is on friendly terms with one or more members of the community. Some swans are relatives of vampires, open and accepting of their nature. Some are club goers who like to dress the part of the vampire, fake fangs and all, but do not in any way claim to be anything other than a "lifestyler." Some are psychics, witches, and  energy manipulators of all sorts who have chosen to embrace the differences between themselves and vampires rather than fear them. Some are perfectly normal, open-minded people who know vampires in their everyday lives and who simply accept them for who they are. Consider the case of the Roma: the entire race has a long-standing friendship with the Strigoi Vii. Of course, more than anyone, the greatest friends of the community, the vampire's most respected and esteemed associates, and those most likely to be confused for vampires, are the blood and energy donors.

Regardless of how much information the vampire community puts out, a certain amount of the human population remains tenaciously convinced that vampirism is something one can catch. So, they believe that those people who give to vampires a small part of themselves are somehow vampiric as well.

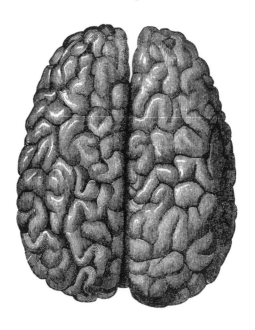

Sociopaths

One in twenty-five Americans is born with a mental condition known as *sociopathy*, sometimes also called *psychopathy*. Though no one really has a clue what causes this condition, it is believed to be caused by an inability of the brain to form love-based bonds with others, which causes a number of side effects that typify sociopathic behaviors. These behaviors include a number of antisocial, even violent, behaviors, and an emotional disconnection even from one's own parents. But the prime behavior—the one that dictates whether a person is classified as a sociopath—is a reduced or nonexistent ability to feel the emotion commonly known as guilt.

Sociopaths have a predatory nature similar to vampires. They have a hunger of their own, an insatiable ambition for power and dominance, so in many ways they are easily mistaken for vampires. But they often get lost in fantasy themselves and begin to believe that they are vampires—a natural and understandable conclusion if one understands how a sociopathic childhood affects a person. So sociopaths really fit into two categories: those who claim to be vampires, and those who are mistaken for vampire kind.

In truth, most sociopaths are not vampiric, but few people would be surprised if it is one day discovered that the vampiric community has a disproportionately high number of sociopathic members. Vampires tend to be independent-minded and fiercely ambitious people, so an intelligent and ethical sociopath would blend in well with them. It is no surprise, then, that closed-minded or simply uneducated humans are fearful of, or even abusive toward, both the vampirically and sociopathically inclined members of society. But one should always keep in mind that as long as the harmful and destructive sides of one's nature are kept in check, even a monster can be a magnificent leader.

False Vampiric Attacks

Over the last few centuries, the Western world has tried to blame many of its fears and hesitations on vampires. Humans blame them for diseases. Humans blame them for crops dying. Vampires are blamed for both natural and supernatural problems and even for the perfectly normal, though sometimes disquieting, workings of their own bodies.

For example, take sleep paralysis. It is a perfectly normal part of every living person's daily routine, and yet some people still remain completely unaware of what it is. Sleep paralysis is, in short, the body's complete inability to move while asleep. A little switch of sorts between the brain and body is flipped when a person goes to sleep, thereby preventing every person in the world from getting up in the middle of the night, or of the day for many, and acting out every insane impulse that passes through his dreaming mind.

Sometimes people wake up too fast. Sometimes the brain becomes alert and aware before the switch can be flipped back into the "on" position. Worse yet, sometimes people continue to dream even as their eyes pop open and they begin to discover that they are fully paralyzed. In this state, the brain literally begins dreaming up explanations for the condition. The resulting hallucinations take on all manner of shapes, but all are dictated by the person's personal beliefs, and all involve an attack of some kind. A Christian might see a bat-winged and fork-tongued demon; a "believer" will likely see her own rendering of the large-eyed, gray-skinned aliens she so adamantly believes are "out there;" and the superstitious and those who are simply afraid of the dark, two groups that seem to have numbered in the thousands during the Middle Ages, seem to prefer hallucinating about vampirically inclined apparitions. In Newfoundland this phenomenon is known as the *old hag*; in the West Indies, *kokma*; in Japan, *kanashibari*; and in China, *gui ya*.

Regardless of what the mind chooses, most of those awake yet still paralyzed and dreaming end up simply falling back asleep and continuing their fantasy in the dream world, allowing the dream to turn into a full alien-abduction story or a detailed encounter with an insatiably violent or lustful vampire, powered by all the fear that a mind in a deeply strange and unfamiliar situation can muster.

Not all nighttime attacks are a result of simple misidentification of natural phenomena, though. Some attacks really are the result of poltergeist activity. The dead are often just as active as the living, and being dead does not change a person's personality. Some people are benevolent and kind, and some people

are manipulative and controlling. In particular, some of the deceased who have no living person to care for them and send them energy, and thus keep them fed, will turn to harmful and malicious behavior to encourage people to direct energy at them. Reacting to this behavior, like reacting to a spoiled child, gives the perpetrator precisely what he wants. Fear, anger, and anxiety are naturally powerful emotions that will flood an environment and nearly circumvent the need for a sympathetic frequency, though a sympathetic frequency does develop as the haunted develop a very personal disdain for the haunter. Naturally, traditional Christian exorcisms never work. Yelling and screaming at a malicious entity and demanding that it be gone only sends more energy its way, no matter how many times a priest invokes the name of his god—though in truth the activity may subside temporarily afterward. Of course, this is not because the exorcism did the spirit any harm but rather because the high-energy emotional process fed it well enough for it to become quite satisfied for a time. And for the poltergeist the real bonus is that the excess energy it now has will allow it to do greater harm to its victims and get an extra boost from the panic, anger, and surprise that are caused by its unexpected and dramatic return.

Some have tried to make the case that these entities are vampiric because they feed on the emotions of the victim. This is simply not so. All spirits are made of electromagnetic energy and therefore must feed on the same energy to survive. Human spirits must be given this energy. It must be projected at them on a sympathetic frequency or in a quantity large enough to bypass the need for a sympathetic frequency, and so if a spirit does not have a living person capable of sending it energy or willing to send the energy, and for whatever reason the spirit is not ready to reincarnate, it must find a way to gain attention.

Vampiric spirits by their very nature do not require attention to feed. Attention can come in handy at times, but it is not necessary. So, even as disembodied spirits—ghosts, if you like—they still simply take what they need from those they choose, with no bad behavior or malicious tricks required. People forget that spirits attack because they are weak and have no other way to get energy. They are pitiful and untalented, not strong or worthy of the fear given to them.

Along with witches and "evil" spirits, vampires were once blamed for crop failures, infertility, and even crib death. If disease struck a home, it was a sure sign that a deceased relative had come back as a vampire, and if a man became impotent, it was obvious his masculine prowess was being drained by nightly visits from a succubus. In some areas, the Black Death itself was blamed on the malicious doings of those creatures of the night, which is ironic considering that certain small areas of Europe favored by the Strigoi Vii remained oddly plague free. One can only imagine that the reason for this is a combination of vampires' natural

propensity toward cleanliness, their balanced energies and use of them to heal themselves and others, and their widespread love of cats—cats that ate the rats that carried the fleas that spread the disease. The more superstitiously prone people of the time were too busy burning the supposedly demonic felines by the bushel to consider the logic of the situation.

In the end, whether a false vampire is claiming to be a real vampire or a natural phenomenon is mistaken for an attack, it is fear that lends these situations credibility. Humans are afraid that there are powerful and malicious spirits out there, great in number and unstoppable in their quest to drain the life from every person they can.

CHAPTER 9

Am I a Vampire?

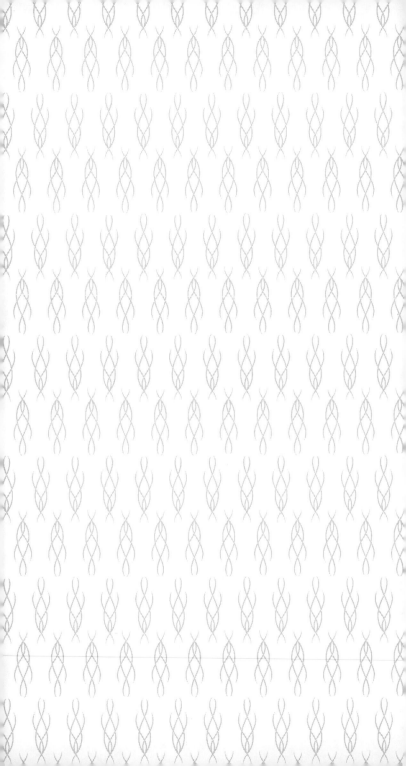

If you have read through all of this book, you have probably already asked yourself whether you are a vampire. Unfortunately, the answer does not come easy: the only person who can answer the question is you. Yes, vampires recognize their own, but asking someone who himself says he is a vampire will provide no final answer. If the person you ask is indeed vampiric, or a talented psychic, she will be able to provide you with the truth, but it may be a truth you are not ready to understand or accept. If the person you ask is not vampiric or particularly psychic but is instead a wannabe or a sympathetic vampire, then he may be able to give you an answer, but it will most likely not be accurate. Truth can be found only within, so trust yourself, and be honest with yourself.

A true vampire can, however, help a person to discover her own vampiric nature. A vampire can provide information about the early warning signs of a vampiric nature, what an Awakening is like, and how to recognize others—all of which this chapter is designed to do as well.

Early Warning Signs

Whether it is you who may be a vampire or you are the parent of a young child who may be one, the first noticeable sign of a vampiric nature is the person's appetite. The Hunger tends to set in pretty early, long before the Awakening begins, so it is not uncommon for the little "changeling" to have an insatiable desire for food. Of course, this is not the typical overeating behavior that children are known for—gobbling down sweets until they become ill. Rather, it is usually a craving for meats especially, but other solid foods, too, as well as a great thirst to match it. It is not a child simply being a little piggy, but an obvious sign that the child's body is using up all its resources too quickly. Sometimes vampiric children become somewhat overweight due to what they eat or a lack of an active lifestyle, but actual obesity is uncommon. Their bodies truly are using the resources they consume to fuel their oversize spirits.

The lack of physical activity that may cause weight gain could be a result of an early onset of sun sensitivity—not a particularly common ailment, but one that occurs among the vampiric young occasionally. The sun-sensitive young will often have trouble seeing well in bright light, perhaps even getting headaches from it, and will always prefer darker environments. They may find that they cannot tan from sunlight and instead only burn, and they have a tendency to overheat and dehydrate easily when simply sitting still in direct sunlight, despite the fact that indoors they may be quite athletic and active.

Sunlight is not the only thing that can cause headaches for the vampiric young. A lack of training in controlling the energies of their powerful spirits will often cause severe buildup of energy in the head, resulting in severe migraines. Migraines are very different from normal headaches. Severe, mind-numbing pain is just the beginning. Light sensitivity can increase exponentially, and blind spots in the vision can develop. A true migraine always lasts for hours at a time, sometimes even for days, and no painkiller really ever helps. Sleep is the only relief, but the pain, so severe that it makes you actually consider clawing out your own eyes, often removes true rest as a possibility.

It is hard to imagine what it must be like for a parent to watch his child completely immobilized by a migraine or hurt by the sun, but worse yet is the emotional problems young vampires have. For the psychically sensitive, the emotional difficulties can change on a daily basis, but for the average young vampire, depression is the most common challenge. Depression in children is not uncommon, but the difference between the average child and a vampiric child is, first, that there is no direct emotional cause. The depression does not set in due to parents getting divorced or a pet dying. It is a result of her entire spirit settling into a state of low power usage, a sort of slowing of the spirit's metabolism. Second, the difference between this vampiric depression and normal emotional depression is its consistency and the length of time that it lasts. A young

vampire may remain in a constant state of depression throughout most of her childhood, and if it sets in early enough, she may not realize she was ever depressed until much later in life, usually after the Awakening.

Am I Awakening?

As mentioned before, an Awakening is basically that point in a vampire's life in which his mind opens up to the possibility that he might be vampiric. This can occur at any age and may not always happen when the vampire first encounters the concept of real vampires. This period usually takes many months, sometimes even years, to completely pass through, and though it hits most like an epiphany, sometimes it comes on much slower. Either way, for the un-Awakened vampire, finding out that there are real vampires in the world often triggers something inside, like a little light clicking on, shedding just a little bit of illumination on a new part of his self that was there all along, waiting to be discovered. Instinctively skeptical, vampires are often slow to admit even to themselves that they are what they are, but that first little bit of information, that first encountering of the concept, triggers a desire to learn more.

For the average vampire, the concept that she might be a vampire often seems natural, though strange and contrary to the ideas of the world she was raised in. Wiccans describe a similar sense of "coming home" when they discuss their first encounters with magick—a simple attunement to a truth the person felt was there all along. For vampires, there is an additional sense of relief when they begin to accept that there was a reason behind all the migraines and oddities, and realize that there may be a solution. The relief does not last long, though. Soon, the changes come.

The entire gamut of vampiric weaknesses and abilities has been there for each vampire throughout the entirety of their un-Awakened lives, but most often in more subtle forms. Once the Awakening begins, the subtlety is stripped away, exposing the young vampire for the first time to the full intensity of his existence.

A change in sensory perception often comes first, leaving the newly Awakened with overly sensitive vision or hearing, which will take them time to learn to cope with. A particular sensitivity to the smell of blood is quite common, due to its rather unique aroma, and on occasion, those with no previously noticeable psychic abilities will suddenly begin to see, feel, or otherwise sense energy flows and auras.

These and other changes are all a result of the vampire simply getting more in touch with her spirit, actively using its power for the first time and becoming hypersensitive to its needs. The vampire will need time to get used to these expanded senses and sensitivities but will eventually find the right internal balance to cope with them.

Finding this internal balance plays a major part in the vampire's ability to sense and manipulate energy; whether the vampire feeds on blood or energy makes little difference. This ability will grow, resulting in what vampires often see as their trademark, the disruption or destruction of electrical equipment—yet another change those Awakening must learn to incorporate into their lives.

Practicing with feeding, particularly for the energy feeders, is another major part of the Awakening. By this point in the Awakening, any true vampire still questioning whether he is or is not vampiric should have this question finally put to rest when he becomes fully aware of those extra energy-based appendages vampires call their feeding tendrils.

It is said that those just developing an awareness of the tendrils feel something like what one would feel were one's own hair moving around underwater, though the tendrils often move with a mind of their own, acting instinctively on the vampire's own emotions and subconscious desires. If a person a vampire dislikes comes too close, the vampire may feel her tendrils harden into a kind of briar patch to drive the person away, and should the vampire find herself near someone she cares for, her tendrils will often wrap themselves around the person in a gentle embrace. Not everyone enjoys this embrace, though, so until the young vampire develops a working control of her "seaweed," she should be mindful to keep her distance from anyone showing any signs of claustrophobia or any other adverse reaction. Those who truly are going through their Awakening simply need to get used to the fact  that some people are going to instinctively dislike their very presence. A true mark of the vampire is the fear she inspires in humanity, whether she wants to or not.

Finding Others

Let us apply the scientific method to the Awakening process. You have proposed the theory that you or someone you know may be vampiric. You have done your research, which has included gathering all the information you could from the Internet, educational television programs, and books like this one. You have tested your hypothesis not once, but multiple times in multiple ways—by, for example, determining how much energy you can take and from how far away, as well as engaging in various forms of energy manipulation, psychic perception, and the use of the tendrils. (If you have not yet experimented with your psychic abilities, you should consult Michelle Belanger's *The Psychic Energy Codex*.)

You have found your results and come to your conclusion. It may not have been the one you expected, but it is there and ready for the final proof. While it still remains a pure and simple truth that only you can determine whether you are or are not a vampire, you now need outside verification, and that means finding other vampires.

The proof comes when a person sees a vampire face-to-face. For those who are true vampires, the beacon is felt for the first time, and along with this feeling comes the simple knowledge that this person is like you, family, and that you are not alone. For those who are not vampiric yet still believe they are, an encounter with a real vampire is often the final truth that shocks them back into reality as they finally accept that they are not, nor could they ever be, a true predator.

Vampires are not "believers" by nature. Throughout their lives they continually test their natures and abilities to ensure that they are not deluding themselves. Anything short of that would be a path toward living in a fantasy world. However, it is not for proof alone that they seek out other vampires. They instinctively seek their own for companionship, a sense of belonging, and the sharing of similar experiences.

Meeting others is not always simple, though. Not all vampires live in big cities with massive populations that increase their chances of running across one another. Not all of them live in open-minded areas where it is safe to display what they are. Sometimes, even in this day and age, not all vampires have access to a computer with which to reach out to others in their area through message boards and other such methods of communication. What are these vampires to do for that final proof?

One can always check out the local library to gain access to a computer and the Internet long enough to look up a few names, dates, and locations of vampiric gatherings and events. The vampire community hosts a number of events throughout the United States and Europe at different times of the year, often during holidays, so there is likely to be at least one event within driving distance. Many newly Awakened vampires are not yet old enough to attend many of these gatherings or to travel alone. What are they to do when meeting others seems totally out of the question?

For those who have access to the Internet or enough television channels to have seen Michelle Belanger or Reverend Crudelia on any number of cable channel specials discussing real vampires, the next best thing to meeting someone in person is watching someone on video—watching him speak and watching him move. A moving body shows so much more than a still image, and with a little practice the feeding tendrils can be seen even in a video capture. Of course, there will always be fakes claiming to be vampiric, but simple logic and wisdom will allow the seeker to sort out the real vampires from the fake ones, and as always, some vampires' tendrils will be easier to see than others'.

Conclusion

Ultimately, the concept of vampires has many facets. For some, the vampire is nothing more than a fiction, a figure of romance or fear to delight or terrify daydreams. To others, the vampire is a cultural archetype, a reflection of the deepest desires that exist in a people's collective mind, showing the world what they truly feel—in essence, an anthropologist's cheat sheet for understanding a culture. And to yet others, vampires are a day-to-day reality, not to be feared or romanticized but to be understood as best one can. Each of these facets has been featured in this compendium to help the reader gain as broad an insight into the world of vampires as possible. This book also functions as a guide to identifying the many types of vampires and understanding their wide and varying practices. To the reader I say, good luck in your studies, be mindful of your surroundings, be respectful of the company you keep, and never forget your field guide.

Glossary

An. The father god of Sumer. He was married to his sister, Ki, and fathered a race of gods called the *Annunaki*. His symbol was the circle of the sun, and he was generally thought to have dominion over the heavens and the spirit world.

Anne Rice. A popular modern fiction writer and the author of a many erotic horror novels. She is most well known for her vampire stories and the ever-popular character Lestat. Several movies have been made from her novels, including *Interview with the Vampire* and *Queen of the Damned*.

Annunaki. The gods of Sumer, descended from An and Ki. Also called the *Nfl*.

asasabansam. A historic vampire of the Ashanti people of central Ghana. Of a general human shape, this metal-toothed creature sat in treetops awaiting prey to snatch up in its hooks, which it had instead of feet. Its legs extended all the way to the forest floor.

astral projection. The act of sending one's spirit out from one's body. It usually occurs while the body sleeps, though it or something similar has been reported to occur while the person is engaged in a repetitious exertion.

Atlanta Vampire Alliance. A vampiric research group base in Atlanta, Georgia.

Awakening. The process in which a person realizes his own nature and begins to accept and understand it. Vampires experience an Awakening when they begin to recognize their vampiric nature and start the process of learning about what they are and what they need.

bajang. The male version of the *langsuir.*

beacon. An innate sense that allows vampires to feel another of their own kind when in close proximity. Vampires claim to feel it as a sense of deep familiarity with the other vampire and of free-flowing energy between the two.

Bela Lugosi. A talented actor who, despite being typecast in horror roles, played in many movies. Most famous for his portrayal of Bram Stoker's character Count Dracula, he died during the filming of the movie *Plan 9 from Outer Space,* which is widely acknowledged as the worst movie ever made.

Black Veil. A code of conduct originally written in 1997 by Father Sebastian of House Sahjaza for the Sanguinarium. It has since been adopted by the wider community and most modern vampire houses. The vampiric community widely accepts these thirteen rules as law. The Veil is comparable to the Wiccan Rede or the Ten Commandments.

blood feeding. The process by which a vampire takes in blood for the purposes of sustaining his life.

blood fetishist. An individual who receives a sexual thrill from interaction with blood. Some claim to be vampires, though few true vampires think of blood as anything more that just food.

Bram Stoker. An Irish author in the late nineteenth and early twentieth century most well known for his vampire fiction, including his book *Dracula*, which has not been out of print since its first publication, more than one hundred years ago.

Buffy the Vampire Slayer. A popular television series based on a movie by the same name. Buffy, played by Sarah Michelle Gellar in the television series, is a teenage girl destined to save the world from demons, warlocks, and, of course, vampires.

Carpathia. A common term for the region surrounding the Carpathian Mountains used by many of the peoples who emigrated from the region.

Celts. The progenitors of the modern peoples of Ireland, Scotland, and most of the other nearby islands. The Celts had rich mythologies and histories and were known for their fierce warriors, beautiful art, and bizarre funerary practices. Their vampire of myth is the Sidhe.

chakra. An energy core of a spirit. Chakras, which operate like organs and can be thought of as spinning balls of energy, are found evenly dispersed throughout the energy body of the spirit. Human and vampire spirits are generally thought to have seven chakras.

changeling. A Sidhe baby who is exchanged with a human baby, to be raised by human parents. The Celtic myth of the changeling likely arose to explain the behavior of young vampires born to human parents, particularly the behavior of the Dhampyri—those who are born Awakened.

Charlaine Harris. The author of the Sookie Stackhouse series of vampire novels, whose main character is a bubbly, persistently optimistic female with a telepathic "handicap." The series began with the book *Dead Until Dark* and has recently been adapted into the HBO series *True Blood*.

Ch'ing Shih. A type of Chinese spirit demon that can take possession of a the body of a person who recently died. These creatures were known to fly through the air and drink the blood of both the living and the dead, after which they always removed the head of the victim.

chupacabra. Also known as the *goat sucker*, this monster of modern Mexican myth takes many forms but always seems to prefer to attack goats. Its existence may be a simple product of creative tabloid journalism.

ciuapipiltin. The *princess* vampire of native Mexican myth. She dwelt at crossroads and was particularly fond of feeding on children owing to the nature of her creation: she died during the birth of her first child.

conscious feeding. The process by which a vampire feeds with full awareness and intention. Conscious feeding provides the only way for a vampire to feed deeply in a short period of time.

deep communion. A feeding from the core energies of a donor. This feeding process is claimed to create a long-lasting or even permanent deep psychic bond.

Dhampyr. A vampire who is born Awakened. These rare individuals usually end up with very eccentric, nonhuman behavior patterns. Some believe that the Dhampyri are the oldest vampire spirits, so old that they are born into every lifetime knowing their nature and needs.

djinn. Commonly known in the West as *genies*, these powerful spirits of Arabic legend are said to have unmatched magical powers. One could win favors from these creatures by freely giving of one's own spiritual energies.

Don Henry. A respected member of the modern vampire community. He gained early fame by participating in a reality experiment on the Sci Fi channel called *Mad Mad House.*

donor. A person who consciously and willingly participates in a vampire's feeding process by donating blood or energy to a vampire. Donors are a precious resource to the vampire community and are generally very well respected.

Dracula. Bram Stoker's famous character, named after Vlad the Impaler. Dracula was likely based upon many known vampires throughout history, perhaps even an actor friend of Stoker's.

dreamwalk. An event in which one individual consciously enters the dreams of another, transmitting information directly to the other person. The most common signs of a dreamwalk are a feeling that a dream seems "realer than real" and that the dreamer cannot control the dream, together with a clear recollection of the entire dream even long after waking. Vampires have been known to use dreamwalks to psychically feed.

Ekimmu. Descendants of the gods An and Ki of Sumer. Generally, these were bodiless spirits who could find no rest and wandered the earth looking for human victims. They were known to lurk in deserted or ill-omened places. Interestingly, Babylonian stories seem to refer to powerful spirits and deities almost interchangeably. This may be because the Babylonians believed that only the descendants of An and Ki could manifest themselves after death, or it may be because they worshiped dead spirits as deities.

electromagnetic field. A field of force associated with a moving electric charge and consisting of electric and magnetic fields that are generated at right angles to each other.

electromagnetic wave. A wave of energy with a frequency within the electromagnetic spectrum, generated by the periodic fluctuation of an electromagnetic field resulting from the acceleration or oscillation of an electric charge. Electromagnetic waves can be reflected, refracted, and polarized, and exhibit interference and diffraction effects.

electromagnetics. The branch of physics concerned with the interaction between electric and magnetic currents.

Elizabeth Bathory, Countess. Ruler of a county in Hungary during the early seventeenth century. Also known as the *Blood Countess,* she was most well known for sadistically torturing young peasant girls and bathing in their blood, believing that the blood had rejuvenating qualities. Her crimson reign was ended when she made the mistake of killing a young noblewoman, thereby drawing the attention of King Matthias II, who sent a team to investigate her actions and ultimately wall her up in her own tower as punishment.

energy feeding. The vampiric taking of energy for the purposes of sustaining the vampire's own life; usually done through the feeding tendrils.

Epic of Gilgamesh. An epic Babylonian tale recounting the life of the hero Gilgamesh.

facade. The human face that vampires show to the world. This mask of humanity is created by smiles, nonthreatening behavior, and a general mimicking of human actions or even thought patterns. Each vampire creates a facade to help them fit in with the masses.

false awakening. The situation in which a human begins feeling the signs of a vampiric Awakening, such as a form of the Hunger, debilitating weakness, nocturnal preferences, inexplicable pain, and predatory instincts. This condition is likely caused by dormant vampiric genetics becoming active because of overexposure to situations that would appeal to a vampire, such as working with blood.

feeding tendrils. Seaweedlike or tentaclelike appendages extending from the spirit of every real vampire. Though primarily designed to facilitate the feeding process, these flexible arms have a number of other uses; they may be used to heal other people, to manipulate energy, or even to physically attack another person.

Fomoire. The warrior caste of the Sidhe. The Fomoire fought against the Tuatha De Danaan in the Second Battle of Mag Tuired.

ghoul. An eater of the flesh of the freshly dead and drinker of the blood of the living, this creature of Arabic myth looked entirely human and tended to live a relatively normal life. It is considered to be a type of djinn.

Gillo. A type of vampire found on the Mediterranean island of Lesbos. Gillos, usually female, would transform into a bird to travel at night and feed. In older stories, transformation into a bird commonly refers to the concept of astral travel or astral projection.

Homo neanderthalus. A primitive species of hominid. The species were hunted to extinction in certain parts of the world by *Homo sapiens,* the direct predecessors of modern humans, *Homo sapiens sapiens.*

House Kheperu. A vampire house highly respected in the vampiric community. The open-minded policies of the house and its excellent public-relations efforts have created a positive image of modern vampires in the human world.

Hunger. The deep need every vampire has to take in energy, whether through blood or through direct energy contact. It takes its name from the fact that it generally feels like a deep hunger or thirst, though no food or drink can sate the need.

hunt. A vampire's search for prey. The hunt can take place anywhere a vampire searches for his food.

incubus. A type of male vampire who primarily feeds through sexual contact. They are often blamed for sleep paralysis.

Jim Butcher. Author of the *Dresden Files* series of novels in which various forms of vampires appear in different vampire "courts," including the White Court, whose members are very similar to modern psychic vampires.

khakhua. The "witch-men" of the Korowai people of Papua New Guinea, these vampiric spirits visit death and disease on the closest relatives of the bodies they inhabit.

Ki. The mother goddess of Sumer. The sister of the god An, her symbol was the flat line of the horizon. She held dominion over the earth and all its inhabitants.

kids in capes. People who falsely claim to be vampiric. Often young, deluded, and looking for a place to belong, these false vampires are usually easy to identify due to their overly dramatic behavior.

Korowai. A native people of Papua New Guinea who regularly practice cannibalism and have a belief in a vampiric spirit called the *khakhua*.

langsuir. A female vampire of Malaysia known to be quite beautiful, with long hair and nails. Fond of sucking the blood of children, she had an additional orifice on the back of her neck which she used to feed. By cutting her nails and hair quite short and stuffing her shucked tresses into the orifice, one could supposedly tame and humanize this lovely vampire.

Lesbos. An island of the Mediterranean known for its female warriors. This is likely the origin of the tales of the Amazons.

Lestat. Anne Rice's famous rock star vampire. He is a perfect example of the modern ideal vampire.

lifestyler. A person who lives the life of a typical romantic vampire, including nocturnal life, Victorian costumes, and fake fangs. Most lifestylers do not claim to be actual vampires, but some do, having gotten carried away in the fantasy.

Lilith. A minor character in the epic tale Gilgamesh, she was adopted by Hebrew mythology as Adam's first wife, only to later be adopted by modern mythology in various forms as the matriarch of all vampires.

loogaroo. A vampire of Grenada who appears as an old woman during the day only to shed its skin at night and travel as a ball of fire as it searches for victims to feed on.

lording. A former practice among the Gypsies of Romania in which one of their own would volunteer to live with a vampire and be the vampire's donor in exchange for the family's safe passage through his dominion.

Lug. The greatest hero of the Tuatha De Danaan during the Second Battle of Mag Tuired. Sired by a Fomoire king himself, Lug was in effect a Sidhe fighting against his own kind, though he was of little value to the Tuatha De Danaan army until he was Awakened by Morrigan.

magick. The conscious use of directed and focused will in an attempt to control and use energies to effect change.

magnetosphere. The region surrounding an astronomical object such as the earth, in which charged particles are trapped and affected by the object's magnetic field. The earth's magnetosphere contains a constant and massive flow of electrons that help to deflect the majority of the sun's damaging ultraviolet radiation.

Matthias Corvinus, King. The king of Hungary during the time of Prince Dracula. Clearly not afraid of the infamous impaler, King Corvinus once had Prince Dracula locked up for three years (or possibly more), only to release him once he had become an ally by marrying into the Corvinus family.

Matthias Corvinus II, King. The king of Hungary during the time of Elizabeth Bathory. He was supposed to have been the one to order an end to her bloody reign.

Michelle Belanger. A well-known and respected Strigoi Vii writer and leader of the vampiric community.

modulation. The process whereby the frequency, amplitude, or another characteristic of a wave is varied in order to transmit information. In conscious spirits, the modulation of electromagnetic waves is how energy is personalized with independent thought.

Moroii. Another term for a Strigoi Vii. This term is Romanian in origin.

Morrigan. A powerful magick user and a Sidhe who abstained from the war between the Fomoire and the Tuatha De Danaan. She gave advice to those who sought it, including Lug, whom she instructed to "Awake." This was likely the first recorded use of the vampiric term *Awaken*.

Nephilim. A race of superhuman beings mentioned in the Christian Bible. They were said to be the product of a mating between an angel and a human, and some believe they were the reason behind Noah's flood. In actuality, these creatures are simply legends based upon stories of the Sumerian gods.

Nia. The baby sister of Piranda and a highly respected member of the Carbone de Travois Gypsy family. Recently deceased, she accomplished many things before her death; she received multiple degrees and doctorates, was a senior member of the Long Beach chapter of the Hell's Angels, and held a fifteen-year professorship at a respected California university. She had no children. She died one week shy of her ninety-eighth birthday, from injuries sustained while bungee jumping.

Nikola Tesla. An inventor and a contemporary of Thomas Edison. His inventions and theories were ahead of his time, and his theory of the wireless transfer of electricity has not only been proved to be true but is also the best scientific understanding of how vampires transfer energy from others into themselves.

obayifo. A vampire of the Ashanti people of central Ghana in West Africa. The *obayifo* were human in form, with no particular sign of their vampiric nature other than their constantly searching eyes and abnormally strong appetites. At night, their spirits left their bodies to feed, emitting a phosphorescent light as they traveled.

Ordo Dracul. The Order of the Dragon, a group of eastern European royalty that both Vlad Dracul and his son Vlad Dracula belonged to. Some believe that this order was made up primarily of Strigoi Vii members.

Penanggalan. A vampire of Malaysia who was nothing but a human head with the stomach sac attached. It sought the blood of newborn infants.

Piranda. A member of the Carbone de Travois Gypsy family, born around the year 1900, who was lorded to a vampire in the summer of 1918. She was lorded several times to the same vampire for the next several years and developed a deep relationship with him before dying of a fever in the mid-1920s.

poltergeist. A German word meaning "noisy ghost." It can be any noisy or disturbing spirit, particularly one that is capable of moving physical objects, though in modern times this term is usually used to refer only to a harmful spirit.

Poppy Z. Brite. The author of a number of Gothic horror novels usually featuring an assortment of creative and eccentric characters. Her popularity grew partly from a cult following of dedicated fans and from her ability to write authentic stories centered in New Orleans, where she has lived for many years.

prey. In vampiric terms, the prey is the human chosen to be fed upon. The prey is not always aware that the vampire is feeding upon it, nor is the prey always a willing participant in the feeding process. Willing participants are called *donors*.

reincarnation. The idea that one spirit will continue on after the death of one body and eventually be reborn into another.

Scota, Queen. The first monarch of the race currently inhabiting Ireland, a race that is properly known as the Scots. The Tuatha De Danaan predicted the arrival of Queen Scota and her two sons, knowing that they would bring destruction. Some believe that this destruction was the return of the Sidhe.

Second Battle of Mag Tuired. An epic tale from Ireland recounting the war between the Tuatha De Danaan and the Fomoire. The most accessible translation of this work is by Elizabeth A. Grey.

Seven Demons. Descendants of the gods An and Ki that appear in Babylonian epic tales, as well as Syrian and Palestinian magic. They were particularly harmful spirits described as "Knowing no mercy, they rage against mankind. They spill their blood like rain, devouring their flesh and sucking their veins."

shield. A general term for any of the various forms of energetic, psychic, and psychological protection. Psychological shields are mental blocks or distractions that allow an individual to protect themselves from things they may find mentally disturbing. Psychical shields are used to protect oneself from a psychic attack. Energy shields are created by flooding energy into the physical world to shield oneself against physical harm; the process is similar to what occurs when a martial-arts master channels their chi into a punch through a stack of bricks.

Sidhe. A vampiric creature commonly known in the Celtic islands (Ireland, Scotland, Wales, England, and the Isle of Man). The origin of the legends of the fairies, the Sidhe were supposed to be beautiful, strong, fair skinned, and unbeatable in battle.

sociopathy. A mental condition that occurs in one in every twenty-five Americans. Sociopaths do not have a conscience and therefore are free of the emotion of guilt. The condition may be a result of a person's not being able to form psychological bonds of love.

Stephenie Meyer. The author of the *Twilight* series of vampire novels. Her first novel, *Twilight*, has had much praise; its vivid insightfulness regarding the concept of vampires suggests the author may have a deep understanding of these creatures.

Strigoi Morte. A term commonly used in Romania and other countries of eastern Europe for a deceased vampire who continues to prey upon the energies of humans long after death.

Strigoi Vii. A term commonly used in Romania and other countries of eastern Europe for a living vampire. The term has been adopted by modern vampires as a more acceptable term for their race.

succubus. A type of female vampire known to feed through sex. They are often blamed for sleep paralysis.

swan. A general term used for people familiar with the vampiric community.

sympathetic vampirism. A condition that occurs when a human being is fed on too much by a vampire, leading to a state in which the human shares some of the vampire's Hunger. A sympathetic vampire will have many of the same characteristics as a vampire, including a sensitivity to sunlight, an insatiable Hunger, nocturnal behavior, and even a craving for blood.

True Blood. A television series on HBO based upon novels by Charlaine Harris and featuring the character Sookie Stackhouse.

Tuatha De Danaan. Generally thought of as gods by the Celtic tribes, this race was most famous for their dubious victory over the seemingly unbeatable Fomoire. They won the Second Battle of Mag Tuired only through underhanded spell casting, back-stabbing, and honorless battle tactics. The story of the battle describes the events by saying "Pride and shame were side-by-side that day."

Twilight series. A series of novels by the Stephenie Meyer, beginning with the novel *Twilight*. Generally aimed at teenage readers though enjoyed by many readers of all ages, the series follows the romantic adventures of the vampire Edward and a human girl, Bella. Meyer's rich and detailed vampiric world includes many clans of vampires, two of which who hunt animals instead of humans, and vampires that sparkle in the sunlight instead of bursting into flames.

unconscious feeding. The process whereby a vampire takes energy in without realizing it. This is common in un-Awakened vampires and in those who feed exclusively on blood.

Uruku. Lesser Babylonian deities descended from An and Ki. Also known as *Utukku*, these disembodied spirits seem to be nearly identical to the Ekimmu except that they generally walk the earth, whereas the Ekimmu are bodyless vampiric spirits. The Uruku are to the Ekimmu what the Strigoi Vii are to the Strigoi Morte.

Vampire: The Masquerade. A role-playing game, produced by the White Wolf company, in which people play the parts of warring vampires. Very popular in the 1990s, the game produced many fiction novels and developed a wide following.

Vlad Dracul, Prince. The father of the famous Dracula and a member of the Ordo Dracul.

Vlad Dracula, Prince. Born in Transylvania in 1431, the son of Vlad Dracul. He is known as a great hero in Romania for his efforts to repel the Turkish invaders, despite his bloody policies, which won him the sobriquet Tepes, or "the Impaler." He was a member of the Ordo Dracul.

whole foods. Solid foods, such as meats, fruits, and vegetables, that are mostly unprocessed, in their natural form, and raised without the use of pesticides.

Wicca. A modern religion based upon ancient polytheistic beliefs. Practitioners usually engage in various forms of magick and energy manipulation. The only belief shared among all Wiccans is the Wiccan Rede: "If it harms none, do as you will."

Bibliography

Belanger, Michelle. *Psychic Dreamwalking: Explorations at the Edge of Self.* San Francisco: Red Wheel/Weiser, 2006.

———. *The Psychic Energy Codex: A Manual for Developing Your Subtle Senses.* San Francisco: Red Wheel/Weiser, 2007.

———. *Vampires in Their Own Words: An Anthology of Vampire Voices.* Woodbury, MN: Llewellyn Publications, 2007.

———. *The Psychic Vampire Codex.* San Francisco: Red Wheel/Weiser, 2004.

Bowes, Susan. *Notions and Potions: A Safe, Practical Guide to Creating Magic & Miracles.* New York: Sterling Publishing Company, 1997.

Budge, E. A. Wallis. *The Book of the Dead: The Papyrus of Ani.* New York: Tess Press, 1895.

Butcher, Jim. *Blood Rites.* New York: ROC, 2004.

———. *White Night.* New York: ROC, 2007.

Dalai Lama. *The Universe in a Single Atom.* New York: Broadway Books, 2005.

Elorath. *Sanguinomicon: Coming Forth by Day.* New York: Lulu.com, 2006.

Greene, Brian. *The Fabric of the Cosmos.* New York: Vintage Books, 2005.

Kaldera, Raven. *The Ethical Psychic Vampire.* Ellhorn Press, 2009.

Konstantinos. *Vampires: The Occult Truth.* St. Paul, MN: Llewellyn Publications, 2005.

McTaggart, Lynne. *The Field.* New York: HarperCollins, 2008.

Raffaele, Paul. *Among the Cannibals: Adventures on the Trail of Man's Darkest Ritual.* New York: HarperCollins, 2008.

Roach, Mary. *Spook: Science Tackles the Afterlife.* New York: W. W. Norton & Company, 2005.

Sebastian, Father. *V.* Amsterdam, Netherlands: *VampyreAlmanac.com*, 2003.

Shadowitz, Albert. *The Electromagnetic Field.* New York: Dover Publications, 1975.

Skal, David J. *Vampires: Encounters with the Undead.* New York: Black Dog & Leventhal Publishers, 2006.

Slater, John C., and Nathanial H. Frank. *Electromagnetism.* New York: Dover Publications, 1947.

Stout, Martha. *The Sociopath Next Door.* New York: Broadway Books, 2005.

Summers, Montague. *The Vampire: His Kith and Kin.* New York: E. P. Dutton and Company, 1929.

———. *The Vampire in Europe.* New York: E. P. Dutton and Company, 1929.

About the Author

Born and raised in the mountains of North Georgia, J. M. Dixon sought answers to the constant oddities pervading his youth from both science and metaphysics. He longs to harmonize the two in an understanding of the natural world. He has every intention of being the first person in history to live forever, while simultaneously living that life to its fullest.

The Weiser
Field Guide Series

For more than fifty years, Weiser Books has published books for seekers and spiritual practitioners from a variety of traditions, from new consciousness to magick to coming earth changes to Western Mystery, Tarot, Astrology, the paranormal, and more. The Weiser Field Guide series developed out of our desire to introduce a new generation of readers and to provide a handbook to esoteric and occult secrets from throughout time and around the world and beyond. We hope these guides entertain and inform.

IN THE SERIES:

The Weiser Field Guide to Ghosts: Apparitions, Sprits, Spectral Lights, and Other Hauntings of History and Legend

The Weiser Field Guide to Vampires: Legends, Practices, and Encounters Old and New

Watch for forthcoming titles.